The Hero Who Restores

Experiencing God's Story Series

The Story Begins: The Authority of the Bible, the Triune God, the Great and Good God

The Hero Who Restores: Humanity, Satan and Sin, Jesus Christ

The Rescue: Salvation, the Holy Spirit, the Church

New People Forever: Transformation, Mission, the End

Experiencing God's Story #2

The Hero Who Restores

Humanity, Satan and Sin, Jesus Christ

J. Scott Duvall

Kregel
Publications

The Hero Who Restores: Humanity, Satan and Sin, Jesus Christ

© 2009 by J. Scott Duvall

Published by Kregel Publications, a division of Kregel, Inc., P.O. Box 2607, Grand Rapids, MI 49501.

This material is also published as part of a workbook under the title *Experiencing God's Story of Life and Hope: A Workbook for Spiritual Formation*, © 2008 and published by Kregel Publications.

ISBN 978-0-8254-2596-7

Printed in the United States of America

09 10 11 12 13 / 5 4 3 2 1

CONTENTS

Acknowledgments   7

Introduction: Read Me First   9

BELIEVING 1   The Weight of Glory: *Humanity*   19

BEHAVING 1   What on Earth Are We Here For? *Seeking the Kingdom*   25

BECOMING 1   Come to Me, All Who Are Weary: *Rest*   29

BELIEVING 2   Not the Way It's Supposed to Be: *Satan and Sin*   34

BEHAVING 2   Our Struggle Is Not Against Flesh and Blood:

                   Waging Spiritual War   40

BECOMING 2   Free at Last, Free at Last: *Freedom*   45

BELIEVING 3   The Word Became Flesh: *Jesus Christ*   49

BEHAVING 3   The Cost of Discipleship: *Following*   54

BECOMING 3   Out with the Old, In with the New: *New Identity*

                   in Christ   58

Works Cited   64

I would like to thank the following people for their help in developing this resource: Brandon O'Brien, Josh and Jill McCarty, Michael and Terese Cox, Julie (Byrum) Stone, Kristine (Lewis) Smith, and Brandon Holiski. The other pastoral leaders at Fellowship Church—Scott Jackson, Neal Nelson, and Darrell Bridges—have been very encouraging throughout the process. My daughter Meagan spent hours sitting in my office punching holes in each page and compiling the first round of books. Thanks, everyone!

Read Me First

Whether you were raised in the church and accepted Christ as your personal savior at age five, or whether you have only recently given your life to Christ, spiritual growth is not optional. God expects his children to *grow up!*

We define *spiritual formation* as the process of allowing God to conform us to the image of Jesus Christ. The Bible clearly teaches that God wants his children to grow to maturity. As you read the sampling of verses below, especially notice the italicized words.

> For those God foreknew he also predestined to be *conformed to the likeness of his Son*, that he might be the firstborn among many brothers. (Rom. 8:29)

> Therefore, I urge you, brothers, in view of God's mercy, to offer your bodies as living sacrifices, holy and pleasing to God—this is your spiritual act of worship. Do not conform any longer to the pattern of this world, but *be transformed* by the renewing of your mind. Then you will be able to test and approve what God's will is—his good, pleasing and perfect will. (Rom. 12:1–2)

> And we, who with unveiled faces all reflect the Lord's glory, are *being transformed into his likeness* with ever-increasing glory, which comes from the Lord, who is the Spirit. (2 Cor. 3:18)

> Therefore we do not lose heart. Though outwardly we are wasting away, yet inwardly *we are being renewed* day by day. (2 Cor. 4:16)

> My dear children, for whom I am again in the pains of childbirth *until Christ is formed in you* . . . (Gal. 4:19)

> You were taught, with regard to your former way of life, to put off your old self, which is being corrupted by its deceitful desires; to *be made new* in the attitude of your minds; and to put on the new self, *created to be like God* in true righteousness and holiness. (Eph. 4:22–24)

. . . being confident of this, that *he who began a good work in you will carry it on to completion* until the day of Christ Jesus. (Phil. 1:6)

Therefore, my dear friends, as you have always obeyed—not only in my presence, but now much more in my absence—continue to *work out your salvation* with fear and trembling, *for it is God who works in you* to will and to act according to his good purpose. (Phil. 2:12–13)

Have nothing to do with godless myths and old wives' tales; rather, *train yourself to be godly.* (1 Tim. 4:7)

Like newborn babies, crave pure spiritual milk, so that by it *you may grow up in your salvation*, now that you have tasted that the Lord is good. (1 Peter 2:2–3)

Each aspect of our definition of *spiritual formation* is significant. Spiritual formation is a *process*. We don't experience growth as a neat, clean, upward slope toward heaven. In reality it looks and feels more like a roller-coaster ride, twisting and turning and looping and climbing and dropping. Only as you stand back and see the big picture can you tell that the "exit" to the ride is higher than the "entrance." Spiritual formation is a messy process. Because we don't always cooperate with the Lord, it takes time for him to accomplish his purpose in our lives. Philippians 1:6 offers a great deal of encouragement here (see above). God never stops working.

Spiritual formation is the process of *allowing* God to work in our lives. God is sovereign but he has also created us to make important decisions and to bear the responsibility for those decisions. We have no power in and of ourselves to cause our own growth, nor will God force us to obey him. We must allow God to work in our lives and to bring about change. God deeply desires to work, but we must give him the necessary time and space. We don't cause our own growth, but we do cooperate with God as he works. Check out Philippians 2:12–13 above.

Spiritual formation is a process of allowing *God* to work in our lives. We are told that the Holy Spirit continues the earthly ministry that Jesus began (Acts 1:1–2). God's Spirit lives within each genuine believer (1 Cor. 6:19). Our growth is not the result of special circumstances or good luck. We don't grow by our own willpower or by striving to obey the Law. We grow when we follow the Holy Spirit, who alone can produce spiritual fruit in our lives (see Gal. 5:16–23). For us to be loving, joyful, peaceful, and so on, the Holy Spirit must be allowed to do his work.

Spiritual formation is the process of allowing God *to conform us* to the image of Jesus. As much as I hate to admit it, growth means change. Like clay in the potter's hand, we are shaped and molded and conformed to a particular pattern. Change at the hand of God is sometimes painful, but it is always good. We don't always like it, but deep down we always desire it because we know it is necessary. James tells us to "consider it pure joy . . . whenever you face trials of many kinds, because you know that the testing of your faith develops perseverance" and "perseverance must finish its work so that you may be mature and complete, not lacking anything" (James 1:2–4). God loves us too much to let us stay as we are.

Finally, spiritual formation is the process of allowing God to conform us *to the image of Jesus Christ*. In Romans 8:29; 2 Corinthians 3:18; and Galatians 4:19 (see page 9), we are told that God is making us more and more like his Son. Jesus is the perfect pattern or model. He represents the goal of spiritual formation. We are not being shaped into merely religious people or ethical people or church-going people. We are being conformed to the very character of Christ himself.

Everyone, without exception, experiences some kind of "spiritual formation." Dallas Willard puts it this way:

> All people undergo a process of spiritual formation. Their spirit is formed, and with it their whole being. . . . Spiritual formation is not something just for especially religious people. No one escapes. The most hardened criminal as well as the most devout of human beings have had a spiritual formation. They have become a certain kind of person. You have had a spiritual formation and I have had one, and it is still ongoing. It is like education: everyone gets one—a good one or a bad one. (*Renovation of the Heart*, 45)

Everyone is being formed by certain powers after a particular pattern or model. We are blessed beyond words to be able to participate in God's design for spiritual formation.

God often uses resources to shape or mold us into conformity with Christ's character. Of course, the primary resource is God's Word, the Bible. But there are also many good and helpful supplementary resources. We certainly know that no ministry resource of any kind can ever substitute for a personal relationship with God through Jesus Christ, but God does seem to use spiritual-growth resources to help our love for him grow deeper and stronger. The Experiencing God's Story series is one particularly effective resource that God can use to help us understand and participate consistently in true, godly spiritual formation.

Believing-Behaving-Becoming

Most resources focus on just one aspect of the spiritual formation process. Some tools emphasize our *beliefs* by explaining the core teachings of the Christian faith. Knowing what to believe is crucial, but there is more. Many spiritual formation resources highlight how we should *behave*. They stress the importance of spiritual disciplines such as prayer, Bible study, solitude, worship, and so on. Without a doubt God uses such disciplines to transform our lives, but the disciplines are means to an end, not the end themselves.

The disciplines are like workout routines pointing toward the game itself. The game is our life with God. Finally, there are a handful of resources that pay attention to what people are *becoming* in the entire process of spiritual formation (i.e., godly character). Most of these center on the fruit of the Spirit as the true test of spirituality, and rightly so.

The Experiencing God's Story series connects all three aspects of spiritual formation: what we believe, how we behave, and who we are becoming. All three are essential to our growth:

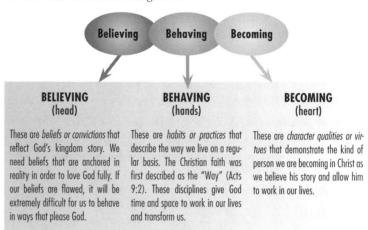

BELIEVING (head)	BEHAVING (hands)	BECOMING (heart)
These are *beliefs or convictions* that reflect God's kingdom story. We need beliefs that are anchored in reality in order to love God fully. If our beliefs are flawed, it will be extremely difficult for us to behave in ways that please God.	These are *habits or practices* that describe the way we live on a regular basis. The Christian faith was first described as the "Way" (Acts 9:2). These disciplines give God time and space to work in our lives and transform us.	These are *character qualities or virtues* that demonstrate the kind of person we are becoming in Christ as we believe his story and allow him to work in our lives.

As a teaching tool, each workbook in this series connects a "Believing" area with a "Behaving" area and a "Becoming" area. Look at the overview on pages 16–17 to see the whole plan. For example, in the third row of the overview you will notice a belief in a great and good God. That belief is connected to the habit of worship and to the quality of purity or holiness. In other words, each row of the overview is connected and integrated; each belief is tied to a behavior or habit and then to a character quality.

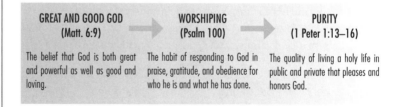

GREAT AND GOOD GOD (Matt. 6:9)	WORSHIPING (Psalm 100)	PURITY (1 Peter 1:13–16)
The belief that God is both great and powerful as well as good and loving.	The habit of responding to God in praise, gratitude, and obedience for who he is and what he has done.	The quality of living a holy life in public and private that pleases and honors God.

This Believing-Behaving-Becoming arrangement is merely a teaching tool and is not intended as a rigid religious system. Sometimes beliefs lead to behavior, while at other times behavior influences beliefs. I'm not suggesting a 1-2-3, neat, clean, foolproof, linear progression that will solve all of life's problems. We all know that life is messy, dynamic, unpredictable, confusing, spontaneous, mystical, and so on. But I still think there are important connections to be made using this teaching arrangement. For instance, what we believe about Satan and sin will affect how we fight spiritual battles and how we understand and experience true freedom. While recognizing this somewhat artificial organization, I hope the Believing-Behaving-Becoming setup encourages you to allow the Lord to work in your entire life rather than just one area of your life.

The four study guides in this series include a total of thirty-six boxes of beliefs, behaviors, and character qualities.

Why these particular topics? Were they chosen simply because they are the most popular topics when it comes to spiritual growth? Are we looking at a random bunch of beliefs and habits and virtues all loosely connected? Actually, the topics were not chosen at random or through some popularity contest. These topics reflect God's story and in our context today we definitely need to stay anchored to God's story.

Experiencing God's Story of Life and Hope

Since the late 1960s we have been experiencing a cultural shift from modernism to postmodernism. (See Jimmy Long's excellent book *Emerging Hope* for more on this cultural change and how Christians can respond.) The modern era emphasized the individual, objective truth, words, and some kind of grand story to explain the meaning of life. By contrast, the postmodern era emphasizes community, subjective "truth," images, and the absence of any grand story to explain life. Christians can embrace some aspects of postmodernism and probably need to resist others. For instance, we can certainly celebrate the greater emphasis on community. But if we give up on a big story that explains reality, then we might as well give up on our faith.

The Christian faith is founded upon God's grand story revealed in the Bible. Postmodernism does away with all big stories that claim to explain reality, opting instead for local or small-group stories. What is true for me and my friends is what is true—period! But Christians can't abandon God's grand story or there is nothing left to believe and all hope is lost. Instead, we need to understand God's story even more and see how it connects to life and how it does us good. We would say that what is real and true is not just what my local group prefers, but what God has revealed. God's story explains life.

Spiritual formation needs to be connected to God's story or it can be manipulated to mean almost anything. In other words, we need a biblical story approach to spiritual formation. But we obviously need to do more than just "believe" the story. We need to act upon the story and allow God's story to shape our whole being. Perhaps now the title makes more sense. We need to experience (beliefs, habits, character qualities) God's story (as revealed in the Bible) of life and hope (a story that does what is best for us).

How is this story approach built into these workbooks? It's simple. If you look again at the overview you will notice that the "Believing" column is actually God's grand story.

BELIEVING	(meaning in the story)
Authority of the Bible	A trustworthy script for the story
Triune God who is Great and Good	Begins with God who is community
Humanity	God wants to share his community
Satan and Sin	Evil powers try to ruin the plan
Jesus Christ	The hero of the story
Salvation	The rescue begins
Holy Spirit	God with us until the end
The Church	The community being rescued
Transformation	God works among his children
Mission	God works through his children
The End	The end—we are with God in the new creation

The very first item in the column is the *Bible* or the script of the story. The story proper begins with *God*—who he is and what he has done. God creates *human beings* to relate to him in perfect community, but *Satan and sin* spoil God's good creation and interfere with his story. God must now attempt a rescue to save his creation. Because of his great love for us, God sent his Son *Jesus Christ* to rescue us from Satan and sin and restore us to a relationship with him. *Salvation* means that God has come to rescue us from the dark side. Through Christ, God offers us a way home. As we respond to his gracious offer by trusting him, we are adopted by God into his family. He puts his very own *Spirit* within us and incorporates us into his community. God desires to use this *new community* (called *church*) to provide us with identity, stability, and wholeness. As we eat, pray, worship, and listen to God's Word together, we begin to feel safe. We open up, revealing our joys and struggles. We discover that we can really be known and loved at the same time, rather than just one or the other. Perhaps for the first time we experience life and hope through Christ and his community. We are *transformed* into the kind of person we were created to be. Naturally, we want other people to experience this life and hope. We have a *mission*— to live out God's story in biblical community so that others can join God's community. Since it is a story of hope, God's story *ends* happily (read Rev. 21:1–4).

To summarize, the "Believing" column is God's grand story. Spiritual formation is anchored in God's story. As we move through the story (from top to bottom), each Belief area extends out (from left to right) to a Behaving and a Becoming area. In this way our whole life is being shaped by the Lord and the entire process is firmly secured to God's story.

Workbook Format

Most of the studies in these workbooks consist of the following elements:

- An introduction that explores the biblical context
- "A Closer Look," to dig deeper into a particular text
- "Crossing the Bridge," to move from the ancient world to our world
- "So What?" to apply what we have discovered in the context of biblical community
- "The Power of Words," to help you understand the meaning of words in the text
- Insightful quotes that inspire reflection and action
- Application questions for your small group
- Cross-references for more Bible exploration
- A "For Deeper Study" recommended reading list

In terms of assumptions, characteristics, and benefits, the Experiencing God's Story series is:

- theologically grounded in the evangelical Christian tradition
- spiritually integrated by connecting believing, behaving, and becoming
- academically reliable through the use of solid biblical scholarship
- pedagogically interactive without being insulting (i.e., you won't find rhetorical fill-in-the-blank questions)
- creatively designed to be used by individuals within the context of biblical community
- practically and realistically arranged into four books, each with 3 three-part chapters

Another subtle characteristic worth mentioning is that the workbooks teach by example how to do responsible Bible study. The move from context to observation to theological principle to application follows the journey model detailed in *Grasping God's Word* by Scott Duvall and Daniel Hays.

May the Lord bless you richly as you allow him to conform you to the image of Jesus Christ. I pray that the Experiencing God's Story series will serve you well on your journey.

Overview of the Experiencing God's Story Series

	BELIEVING	BEHAVING	BECOMING
The Story Begins	**Authority of the Bible** (2 Tim. 3:16–17) The belief that the Bible is God's inspired Word given to us to help us mature in our faith.	**Studying the Bible** (2 Tim. 2:15) The habit of reading, interpreting, and applying the Bible as the primary means of listening to God.	**Truth** (Eph. 4:20–25) The quality of living and speaking truthfully in a world of lies and deception.
	Triune God (Gal. 4:4–6) The belief that the Bible teaches the triune (three-in-one) nature of God.	**Fellowshiping** (Acts 2:42–47) The habit of living in authentic relationship with and dependence upon other followers of Jesus.	**Love** (1 John 4:7–8) The quality of choosing to do what God says is best for another person.
	Great and Good God (Matt. 6:9) The belief that God is both great and powerful as well as good and loving.	**Worshiping** (Psalm 100) The habit of responding to God in praise, gratitude, and obedience for who he is and what he has done.	**Purity** (1 Peter 1:13–16) The quality of living a holy life in public and private that pleases and honors God.
The Hero Who Restores	**Humanity** (Gen. 1:26–28) The belief that human beings are uniquely created in the image of God.	**Seeking the Kingdom** (Matt. 6:33) The habit of acknowledging that God is our Creator and that we are creatures intended to seek him and his purposes.	**Rest** (Matt. 11:28–30) The quality of living with a deep awareness of and contentment with God's purpose for our lives.
	Satan and Sin (Gen. 3:1–7) The belief that Satan is the leader of the opposition against God and his people, and that all human beings have a willful opposition to God's claim on their lives (sin).	**Waging Spiritual War** (Matt. 4:1–11) The habit of knowing and using appropriate strategies for fighting against the Devil, the flesh, and the world.	**Freedom** (Rom. 8:1–4) The quality of experiencing freedom from Satan's power and sin's domination and freedom for new life with God.
	Jesus Christ (John 1:1–3, 14, 18) The belief that Jesus Christ is God the Son, fully divine and fully human.	**Following** (Mark 8:34–38) The habit of daily choosing to follow Jesus Christ as Lord in every area of life.	**New Identity in Christ** (John 21:15–23) The quality of single-minded allegiance to Jesus Christ above every other competing loyalty.

INTRODUCTION

BELIEVING	BEHAVING	BECOMING
Salvation (Eph. 2:8–10) The belief that salvation is by grace (source), through faith (means), for good works (result).	**Trusting and Acting** (Phil. 2:12–13) The habit of allowing God to work in our lives so that our faith results in action (not salvation by works, but true faith that works).	**Assurance** (Rom. 8:15–16) The quality of knowing (with a healthy confidence) that we belong to God.
Holy Spirit (John 14:16–17) The belief that God the Spirit continues Jesus' earthly ministry, especially that of transforming believers and empowering them to fulfill their mission.	**Walking by the Spirit** (Gal. 5:16, 25) The habit of living in dependence upon the Holy Spirit as the source of strength to resist temptation and imitate Jesus Christ.	**Fruit of the Spirit** (Gal. 5:22–24) The quality of bearing the fruit of the Holy Spirit (Christlike character qualities) in one's life.
The Church (1 Peter 2:4–10) The belief that God's people are joined together in Christ into a new community, the church.	**Serving** (Mark 10:35–45) The habit of being a servant to other members of this new community.	**Humility** (Luke 18:9–14) The quality of a servant's attitude grounded in the recognition of our status before God and our relationship to others.
Transformation (Rom. 12:1–2) The belief that we are not to be conformed to this world, but we are to be transformed into the image of Jesus Christ.	**Praying** (Matt. 6:9–13) The habit of continual communion with God that fosters our relationship and allows for genuine transformation in our lives.	**Peace** (Phil. 4:6–7) The quality of calmness and well being (vs. worry and inner turmoil) that comes as a result of our communion with God.
Mission (Matt. 28:18–20) The belief that Jesus commissioned his church to make disciples of all nations.	**Engaging the World** (Acts 1:7–8) The habit of engaging the world for the purpose of sharing the good news of Jesus Christ.	**Compassion** (Luke 10:30–37) The quality of extending love and compassion to people in need.
The End (1 Thess. 4:13–18) The belief that Jesus Christ will return to judge evil, restore his creation, and live forever in intimate fellowship with his people.	**Persevering** (Heb. 12:1–2) The habit of enduring and persisting in spite of the trials and difficulties we face in life.	**Hope** (Rom. 8:22–25) The quality of a confident expectation that in the end God will be true to his word and keep his promises.

The Rescue

New People Forever

The Weight of Glory

Humanity

36 Life Essentials

BELIEVING
Authority of the Bible
Triune God
Great and Good God
➤ **Humanity**
Satan and Sin
Jesus Christ
Salvation
Holy Spirit
The Church
Transformation
Mission
The End

BEHAVING
Studying the Bible
Fellowshiping
Worshiping
Seeking the Kingdom
Waging Spiritual War
Following
Trusting and Acting
Walking by the Spirit
Serving
Praying
Engaging the World
Persevering

BECOMING
Truth
Love
Purity
Rest
Freedom
New Identity in Christ
Assurance
Fruit of the Spirit
Humility
Peace
Compassion
Hope

In *The Story Begins*, the first workbook in the Experiencing God's Story series, we looked at the Bible as God's inspired Word, our need to study the Bible, and the resulting virtues of truth telling and truth living. Next, we explored the mysterious but amazing conviction that God is Trinity—Father, Son, and Spirit living in an eternal relationship of self-giving love. When we accept God's offer to join his community or fellowship, we begin to allow his love to define our lives. We continued our journey by thinking about God as both good and great, a conviction that calls for a response of authentic worship—a practice that cultivates in us the quality of holiness or purity. The next page in God's grand story moves the focus from God himself to his most precious creation—human beings. Because we have been created in the image of God, we bear an enormous "weight of glory" as C. S. Lewis explains:

> It may be possible for each to think too much of his own potential glory hereafter; it is hardly possible for him to think too often or too deeply about that of his neighbour. The load, or weight, or burden of my neighbour's glory should be laid on my back, a load so heavy that only humility can carry it, and the backs of the proud will be broken. It is a serious thing to live in a society of possible gods and goddesses, to remember that the dullest and most uninteresting person you can talk to may one day be a creature which, if you saw it now, you would be strongly tempted to worship, or else a horror and a corruption such as you now meet, if at all, only in a nightmare. All day long we are, in some degree, helping each other to one or other of these destinations. . . . There are no *ordinary* people. You have never talked to a mere mortal. Nations, cultures, arts, civilizations—these are mortal, and their life is to ours as the life of a gnat. But it is immortals whom we joke with, work with, marry, snub and exploit—immortal horrors or everlasting splendours. (*The Weight of Glory*, 45–46)

The "weight" or "burden" of glory is Lewis's memorable way of describing the biblical conviction that human beings have been created in the image of God.

"image and likeness"—Older biblical scholarship believed that "image" and "likeness" were different. They claimed that "image" referred to the characteristics of personhood that remained after Adam and Eve sinned, while the "likeness" was destroyed by sin. Recent (and better) biblical scholarship says that these two parallel words are communicating a single idea—humans bear God's stamp. We were created with some capacity to mirror God, to be and act like him. We were made in his image or likeness.

SCRIPTURE NOTES

Made in God's Image

Although there are only a few Scriptures that assert that we have been created in God's image, they are crystal clear and powerful.

> When God created man, he made him in the likeness of God. He created them male and female and blessed them. And when they were created, he called them "man." (Gen. 5:1b–2)

> Whoever sheds the blood of man, by man shall his blood be shed; for in the image of God has God made man. (Gen. 9:6)

> With the tongue we praise our Lord and Father, and with it we curse men, who have been made in God's likeness. Out of the same mouth come praise and cursing. My brothers, this should not be. (James 3:9–10)

A Closer Look—Genesis 1:26–28

To these three we add our focal passage for this study:

> 26Then God said, "Let us make man in our *image*, in our *likeness*, and let them rule over the fish of the sea and the birds of the air, over the livestock, over all the earth, and over all the creatures that move along the ground."
>
> 27So God created man in his own *image*,
>
> in the *image* of God he created him;
>
> male and female he created them.
>
> 28God blessed them and said to them, "Be fruitful and increase in number; fill the earth and subdue it. Rule over the fish of the sea and the birds of the air and over every living creature that moves on the ground."

The three image-of-God passages in Genesis occur at very significant points in the story.

- Genesis 1—the high point of creation;
- Genesis 5—the new start following Adam and Eve's fall into sin;
- Genesis 9—the new beginning after the judgment of the flood.

These locations tell us that the "image of God" is crucial to God's plan and vital for us to understand. Since the Bible never explicitly tells us what the "image" is, there have been many attempts to define the "image" (too many to list here). Rather than trying to define what the image is, we are better off looking at what the image involves. For example, what privileges or responsibilities does it carry? As humans made in God's image, what are we supposed to do or not do? Use the questions below to help you get a better feel for what the image of God involves.

1. What does Genesis 1:26–28 suggest that the image of God involves?

2. What do you learn about the image of God from the surrounding context (Genesis 1–2)?

3. As you look at Genesis 5 and 9 and James 3, what do you learn about the image of God?

Crossing the Bridge

Remember, we cross the bridge from the ancient world to our world by identifying timeless theological truths that God is communicating. Here are a few principles related to the image of God. Be careful; taking these truths seriously will radically change your life.

- *All human beings (not just Christians) have value and dignity.* We are important because of who we are (created as important by God). We are not the mere products of naturalistic evolution. People deserve respect, and human life should be regarded as sacred.

Not Worthless, Only Lost

G. K. Chesterton somewhere says that the hardest thing to accept in the Christian religion is the great value it places upon the individual soul. Still older Christian writers used to say that God has hidden the majesty of the human soul from us to prevent our being ruined by vanity. This explains why even in its ruined [or sinful] condition a human being is regarded by God as something immensely worth saving. Sin does not make it worthless, but only lost.

—Dallas Willard, *Renovation of the Heart,* 46

So the spies questioned him: "Teacher, we know that you speak and teach what is right, and that you do not show partiality but teach the way of God in accordance with the truth. Is it right for us to pay taxes to Caesar or not?" He saw through their duplicity and said to them, "Show me a denarius [a Roman coin]. Whose portrait and inscription are on it?" "Caesar's," they replied. He said to them, "Then give to Caesar what is Caesar's, and to God what is God's."

—Luke 20:21–25

What does Jesus' response to the tricksters teach us about the image of God?

?

Feeling Blue?

If you are feeling discouraged, read Psalm 8. To our surprise, God thinks highly of us.

When I consider your heavens, the work of your fingers, the moon and the stars, which you have set in place, what is man that you are mindful of him, the son of man that you care for him? You made him a little lower than the heavenly beings and crowned him with glory and honor. You made him ruler over the works of your hands; you put everything under his feet: all flocks and herds, and the beasts of the field, the birds of the air, and the fish of the sea, all that swim the paths of the seas.

—Psalm 8:3–8

- *We belong to God.* We are not our own. We need God and will only find our ultimate fulfillment in God. We were meant to be God's, not gods.
- *We were created for relationships and community.* If we have been created in the image of the triune God who enjoys an eternal fellowship of love, then we too need relationships—with God and other human beings.
- *We have been granted both freedom and responsibility.* We are charged with "ruling" and "subduing" creation (Gen. 1:28). We are free to make real choices that affect the direction and destiny of our lives and others' lives. God intends for us to cooperate with him in faithfully managing creation.
- *We have been created male and female.* In an age of gender confusion, we need to know how important gender clarity is to God. We are created to live as either male or female and to interact with the other gender in a complementary partnership.
- *Sin may distort the image, but it does not destroy it.* Even after human beings chose to sin, they were told not to kill (Gen. 9) or curse (James 3) people because they have been made in God's image.
- *The image of God is perfectly manifested in Jesus Christ.*

  The god of this age has blinded the minds of unbelievers, so that they cannot see the light of the gospel of the glory of Christ, who is the image of God. (2 Cor. 4:4)

  He is the image of the invisible God. (Col. 1:15)

  The Son is the radiance of God's glory and the exact representation of his being. (Heb. 1:3)

- *Christ followers are renewed in the image of God.* As a result of our relationship with Jesus Christ, the image of God given at creation is being renewed and restored in us.

  For those God foreknew he also predestined to be conformed to the likeness of his Son, that he might be the firstborn among many brothers. (Rom. 8:29)

  And we, who with unveiled faces all reflect the Lord's glory, are being transformed into his likeness with ever-increasing glory, which comes from the Lord, who is the Spirit. (2 Cor. 3:18)

  You were taught, with regard to your former way of life, to put off your old self, which is being corrupted by its deceitful desires; to be made new in the attitude of your minds; and to put on the new self, created to be like God in true righteousness and holiness. (Eph. 4:22–24)

Do not lie to each other, since you have taken off your old self with its practices and have put on the new self, which is being renewed in knowledge in the image of its Creator. (Col. 3:9–10)

When God created us in his image, he gave us dignity and value, entrusted us with significant freedom and responsibility, and gave us the privilege of relating to him. In Christ, the image of God is being restored in us. In sum, in Christ we are becoming fully human!

Brennan Manning tells a story about Ed Farrell, who traveled from his home in the United States to spend two weeks with his uncle, who lived in Ireland. His uncle was celebrating his eightieth birthday. Early on the morning of his birthday, Ed and his uncle took a walk along the shore of Lake Killarney, enjoying the beautiful scenery. For twenty minutes they walked in silence, captivated by the moment. Then his uncle began to do a strange thing for an eighty-year-old man—he began to skip along the shore like a young boy. When Ed caught up with him, he asked, "Uncle Seamus, you look very happy. Do you want to tell me why?" "Yes," said the old man, his face covered in tears. "You see, the Father is very fond of me. Ah, me Father is so very fond of me" (Manning, *Wisdom of Tenderness*, 25–26). Do you get it? The God who created you in his image is very fond of you!

So What?

1. Describe what you assume God thinks or feels when he thinks about you.

2. Is there anything that keeps you from realizing (with both your mind and your heart) that the Father is very fond of you?

Admitting Our Limits

We aren't God and *never* will be. We are humans. It is when we try to be God that we end up most like Satan, who desired the same thing. We accept our humanity intellectually, but not emotionally. When faced with our own limitations, we react with irritation, anger, and resentment. We want to be taller (or shorter), smarter, stronger, more talented, more beautiful, and wealthier. We want to have it all and do it all, and we become upset when it doesn't happen. Then when we notice that God gave others characteristics we don't have, we respond with envy, jealousy, and self-pity.

—Rick Warren,
Purpose-Driven Life, 79

Cross-References

Look back over the references cited throughout Believing 1.

For Deeper Study

Gushee, David P. *Only Human.* San Francisco: Jossey-Bass, 2005.

Lewis, C. S., *The Weight of Glory.* 1949. San Francisco: HarperSanFranciso, 1980.

Sherlock, Charles. *The Doctrine of Humanity.* Downers Grove, IL: InterVarsity Press, 1996.

Walton, John H. *Genesis.* NIV Application Commentary. Grand Rapids: Zondervan, 2001.

Wilkins, Michael J. *In His Image: Reflecting Christ in Everyday Life.* Colorado Springs: NavPress, 1997.

Willard, Dallas. *Renovation of the Heart.* Colorado Springs: NavPress, 2002.

3. Does your primary identity in life come from God's estimation of you or from another source? Explain.

4. Acknowledging our humanity means accepting God's love, admitting that we have limits, cultivating godly relationships, learning how to use freedom, taking responsibility and developing a healthy understanding of human sexuality, just to name a few things. In what way is the Spirit leading you to acknowledge your humanity right now in your life?

5. What can we do as a community of Christ followers to remind each other of how important we are to God?

What on Earth Are We Here For?

Seeking the Kingdom

36 Life Essentials

BELIEVING
Authority of the Bible
Triune God
Great and Good God
Humanity
Satan and Sin
Jesus Christ
Salvation
Holy Spirit
The Church
Transformation
Mission
The End

BEHAVING
Studying the Bible
Fellowshiping
Worshiping
➤ **Seeking the Kingdom**
Waging Spiritual War
Following
Trusting and Acting
Walking by the Spirit
Serving
Praying
Engaging the World
Persevering

BECOMING
Truth
Love
Purity
Rest
Freedom
New Identity in Christ
Assurance
Fruit of the Spirit
Humility
Peace
Compassion
Hope

Because God created us in his image, we are loaded with value and importance. We are free to choose but entrusted with responsibility. We are male or female. We were created to live in community. We belong to God and need God in order to be fully alive human beings. God's original plan for creating us in his image can be fulfilled only in Jesus Christ, who is able to restore the image of God in us.

This glory of being created in God's image carries enormous weight. (Life is tough when you're important!) Some people can't handle the significance of being a valuable human being, so they squander the blessing. In other words, they forget about God and pursue their own selfish agendas. In Behaving 1 Jesus tells us how to make the most of being an image bearer by seeking God and his purposes for our lives. Because we have been created in God's image, we have important work to do—kingdom work.

Although not flashy or famous, Rick Warren's father faithfully imaged his heavenly Father.

My father was a minister for over fifty years, serving mostly in small, rural churches. He was a simple preacher, but he was a man with a mission. His favorite activity was taking teams of volunteers overseas to build church buildings for small congregations. In his lifetime, Dad built over 150 churches around the world.

In 1999, my father died of cancer. In the final week of his life the disease kept him awake in a semi-conscious state nearly twenty-four hours a day. As he dreamed, he'd talk out loud about what he was dreaming. Sitting by his bedside, I learned a lot about my dad by just listening to his dreams. He relived one church building project after another.

"first"—This refers to what is of first importance (i.e., "above all else"), rather than first in time, like the first item on a long list of equally important items. God's kingdom and righteousness are on a list by themselves.

"kingdom"—God's rule or reign that is present now in Jesus Christ (and those who belong to him) and will be fully realized when Christ returns to establish his eternal kingdom.

"righteousness"—Right relationship with God that comes through Christ's saving work, as well as the godly conduct and behavior that comes as the only right response to God's gracious work.

Do What You Are

Usually when we meet someone for the first time, it isn't long before we ask, "What do you do?" ... Work takes up so many of our waking hours that our jobs come to define us and give us our identities. We become what we do.

Calling reverses such thinking. A sense of calling should precede a choice of job and career, and the main way to discover calling is along the line of what we are each created and gifted to be. Instead of "You are what you do," calling says, "Do what you are."

—Os Guinness, *The Call*, 46

One night near the end, while my wife, my niece, and I were by his side, Dad suddenly became very active and tried to get out of bed. Of course, he was too weak, and my wife insisted he lay back down. But he persisted in trying to get out of bed, so my wife finally asked, "Jimmy, what are you trying to do?" He replied, "Got to save one more for Jesus! Got to save one more for Jesus! Got to save one more for Jesus!" He began to repeat that phrase over and over.

During the next hour, he said the phrase probably a hundred times. "Got to save one more for Jesus!" As I sat by his bed with tears flowing down my cheeks, I bowed my head to thank God for my dad's faith. At that moment Dad reached out and placed his frail hand on my head and said, as if commissioning me, "Save one more for Jesus! Save one more for Jesus!" (*Purpose-Driven Life*, 287).

Jimmy Warren was a man who knew God's purpose for his life and embraced it fully.

Career or Calling?

In his book *The Will of God as a Way of Life,* Jerry Sittser defines a *career* as a particular line of work that requires education or training, earns an income, and keeps our society running. A *calling*, on the other hand, is a person's specific, God-given purpose for living. Our calling refers to the way God wants us to use our time, energy, resources, and abilities to carry out his purposes in this world. Rick Warren's father used his career as a small-church pastor to carry out his life calling of leading people to faith in Christ. Here are some other ways to use a career to live out a life calling (see *Will of God*, 165–68):

- "Managing a sporting goods store is a career; challenging people to use their leisure time to find refreshment and renewal is a calling."
- "Teaching social studies at a junior high is a career; providing instruction, support, and guidance to adolescents going through a difficult passage in life is a calling."
- "Functioning as a secretary is a career; organizing an office so that details are handled efficiently, but never at the expense of people, is a calling."

The primary calling of every believer is to trust and obey Jesus Christ, but God seems to call individual believers to specific responsibilities in his kingdom. Our individual calling will grow out of our gifts, abilities, personality, and life experiences. Too often we confuse career and calling, but they are not the same. Our calling is much more important.

A career causes people to think of income, power, position, and prestige. A calling inspires people to consider human need, moral standards, and a larger perspective. A career does not define a person, nor does it determine a calling. If anything, the opposite occurs. God defines the person and gives that person a calling. Then he or she is free to use a career for God's kingdom purpose. (Sittser, *Will of God*, 166)

A Closer Look—Matthew 6:33

The belief that God is our Creator and we are creatures made in his image leads to the habit of seeking him and his purposes as our highest ambition in life. When we talk about life purpose, we are talking much more about calling than career. Jesus gets to the point in Matthew 6:33.

But

seek first his kingdom and his righteousness,

and

all these things will be given to you as well.

1. Take a moment and look carefully at this verse, noting any contrasts, commands, important pronouns, promises, and so on. Mark your observations in the space above.

2. What is the major theme of the section that contains 6:33?

3. The word "but" that begins verse 33 signals a contrast between seeking God's kingdom and what?

4. What does the phrase "all these things" refer back to?

Crossing the Bridge

In this passage, what are the differences between the biblical audience and us?

Higher Loves

Jesus commands us to turn our backs on the god Possession and to turn our primary attention to the quest for the Father's royalty and righteousness. This is not a counsel to seek "spiritual" things instead of material things, or inward things instead of outward things; it is counsel to seek God's things rather than our own.... Jesus creates higher loves in us in order to drive out the lower loves.

—F. D. Bruner, *Christbook*, 268

"All These Things"?

What happens when God's promise to meet the basic needs of Christians seems to go unfulfilled and his people experience starvation? One possible solution is that God expects to fulfill this promise through his people.

When God's people corporately seek first his priorities, they will by definition take care of the needy in their fellowships. When one considers that over 50 percent of all believers now live in the Two-Thirds World and that a substantial majority of those believers live below what we would consider the poverty line, a huge challenge to First-World Christians emerges. Without a doubt, most individual and church budgets need drastic realignment in terms of what Christians spend on themselves versus what they spend on others.

—Craig Blomberg, *Matthew*, 126–27

As you cross from the ancient world to our world, what are the timeless theological truths that Jesus is communicating in Matthew 6:33? (Remember, theological principles should apply equally well to the biblical audience and to us.)

So What?

1. What does being created in the image of God (Gen. 1:26–28) have to do with seeking first God's kingdom and righteousness (Matt. 6:33)?

2. What is your controlling drive, your ultimate quest, your greatest passion? What do you spend most of your time and energy seeking?

3. In one or two sentences write out your life calling. Why has God put you on this earth?

4. What are some careers that could help you fulfill your life calling?

5. Is it necessary to have a career related to your calling?

Seek First the Kingdom

God's kingdom is Jesus Christ ruling over his people in total blessing and total demand. To "seek first" this kingdom is to desire as of first importance the spread of the reign of Jesus Christ. Such a desire will start with ourselves, until every single department of our life—home, marriage and family, personal morality, professional life and business ethics, bank balance, tax returns, life-style, citizenship—is joyfully and freely submissive to Christ.

—John Stott, *Message of the Sermon on the Mount*, 170

Cross-References

Ps. 37; Matt. 6:9–13; 7:24–27; Luke 12:13–34; 16:19–31; 1 Cor. 15:58; Col. 3:23; 1 Tim. 6:17–19

For Deeper Study

Guinness, Os. *The Call: Finding and Fulfilling the Central Purpose of Your Life*. Nashville: Word, 1998.

Packer, J. I. *God's Plans for You*. Wheaton, IL: Crossway, 2001.

Sittser, Gerald L. *The Will of God as a Way of Life: Finding and Following the Will of God*. Grand Rapids: Zondervan, 2000.

Warren, Rick. *The Purpose-Driven Life*. Grand Rapids: Zondervan, 2002.

Come to Me, All Who Are Weary

Rest

Yes, we've been created in the image of God and called to seek his kingdom. God says, "You're important and I have something important for you to do." We have been hardwired for abounding in "the work of the Lord" (1 Cor. 15:58). Deep down we want to live out God's calling with passion and fervor. We want to pursue our kingdom assignment with a radical devotion and wholehearted abandonment, pouring out our lives as an offering to the Lord. We want to do all that, but we're weak and sinful human beings who lose focus and lose sleep and sometimes spin ourselves into a chronic state of exhaustion and discouragement. There should be a partnership between zealous work and intentional rest (John 15). To glorify God we must not only work with all our hearts, but also learn to rest for the sake of our souls. In Becoming 1, we will learn about the much-needed (but often neglected) character quality of rest.

Take a moment and read Matthew 11:20–24 and 12:1–14 (skip over 11:25–30 for now). What do these two sections have in common (hint: a certain response to Jesus)?

36 Life Essentials

BELIEVING
Authority of the Bible
Triune God
Great and Good God
Humanity
Satan and Sin
Jesus Christ
Salvation
Holy Spirit
The Church
Transformation
Mission
The End

BEHAVING
Studying the Bible
Fellowshiping
Worshiping
Seeking the Kingdom
Waging Spiritual War
Following
Trusting and Acting
Walking by the Spirit
Serving
Praying
Engaging the World
Persevering

BECOMING
Truth
Love
Purity
➤ **Rest**
Freedom
New Identity in Christ
Assurance
Fruit of the Spirit
Humility
Peace
Compassion
Hope

SCRIPTURE NOTES

Now read Matthew 11:25–30. How does this section differ from the two surrounding sections (hint: a certain response to Jesus)?

In 11:25–30 we see that it is not the "important" people who respond positively to Jesus but the little children and the weary and burdened. For those who submit to his "yoke," Jesus offers "rest." Let's take a closer look at Matthew 11:28–30.

A Closer Look—Matthew 11:28–30

28Come to me, all you who are weary and burdened,

and I will give you rest.

29Take my yoke upon you and learn from me,

for I am gentle and humble in heart,

and you will find rest for your souls.

30For my yoke is easy and my burden is light.

1. What are the three commands in this passage?

2. What is the tone of these three commands?

3. What kind of people are invited to carry out these commands?

4. What promises are attached to the commands?

5. Circle every reference to Jesus ("I," "me," "my") in the passage on page 30. Why is it so important that Jesus gives personal commands (e.g., "Come to *me*")?

6. As you read the passage carefully, what other significant things do you see?

The most explicit promise in this passage is that those who come to Jesus will find rest. What does this mean? The New Testament speaks of *rest* in at least three different ways.

1. Physical rest

   Then, because so many people were coming and going that they did not even have a chance to eat, he said to them, "Come with me by yourselves to a quiet place and get some rest." (Mark 6:31)

2. Spiritual or relational rest

   By all this we are encouraged. In addition to our own encouragement, we were especially delighted to see how happy Titus was, because his spirit has been refreshed [given rest] by all of you. (2 Cor. 7:13)

3. Eternal rest

   There remains, then, a Sabbath-rest for the people of God; for anyone who enters God's rest also rests from his own work, just as God did from his. Let us, therefore, make every effort to enter that rest, so that no one will fall by following their example of disobedience. (Heb. 4:9–11)

Jesus invites us to come to him to experience a holistic rest that includes all of the above.

"I Can Do All Things . . ."

In running and swimming, we continue to break old records nearly every year. . . . But there must be an end to this, true? We cannot run the mile in one second. . . . There is a built-in physiological limit beyond which records will rarely be broken. So it is in life. We are not infinite. The day does not have more than twenty-four hours. We do not have an inexhaustible source of human energy. We cannot keep running on empty. Limits are real, and despite what some Stoics might think, limits are not the enemy. Overloading is the enemy. Some will respond: "I can do all things through Christ who strengthens me." Can you? Can you fly? Can you go six months without eating? Neither can you live a healthy life chronically overloaded. God did not intend this verse to represent a negation of life-balance. Jesus did not heal all, He did not minister to all, He did not visit all, and He did not teach all. He did not work twenty-hour ministry days. It is God the Creator who made limits, and it is the same God who placed them within us for our protection. We exceed them at our peril.

—Richard Swenson, *Margin*, 77

Crossing the Bridge

Although we are not usually tempted to submit to Old Testament Law, are we sometimes "wearied" and "burdened" by religious regulations forced on us from the outside? Can you think of examples in your life?

Jesus invites people who are overwhelmed (by life, religion, etc.) to come to him and take his burden upon them. The scribes and Pharisees of Jesus' day were putting heavy burdens on people. In Luke 11:46 Jesus says, "And you experts in the law, woe to you, because you load people down with burdens they can hardly carry, and you yourselves will not lift one finger to help them." Yet we know that the "yoke" is a symbol of work and authority, not of ease and lawlessness. We need to be reminded that "Jesus' yoke is not lighter because he demands less, but because he bears more of the load with the burdened" (Keener, *Matthew*, 349). Jesus offers work that is refreshing and good because the Holy Spirit gives strength. Following Jesus means a whole new way of living and bearing responsibilities. He is our gentle and humble teacher who leads by example (cf. Phil. 2).

What other theological principles do you see in Matthew 11:28–30?

So What?

1. How does physical rest relate to emotional and spiritual rest?

2. How would you say you are doing when it comes to balancing "abounding" (working) and "abiding" (resting)?

3. Why does our culture seem to place more value on abounding than on abiding?

Cross-References
Gen. 2:3; Exod. 23:12; 33:14; Ps. 116:7; Jer. 6:16; Acts 15:10; Gal. 5:1; Heb. 4:1–13; 1 John 5:3; Rev. 14:13

For Deeper Study
Buchanan, Mark. *The Rest of God: Restoring Your Soul by Restoring Sabbath.* Nashville: W Publishing Group, 2006.

Hughes, Kent R. *Liberating Ministry from the Success Syndrome.* Wheaton, IL: Crossway, 2008.

Kuhatschek, Jack. *The Superman Syndrome.* Grand Rapids: Zondervan, 1995.

Swenson, Richard A. *Margin.* Colorado Springs: NavPress, 1992.

Webster, Doug. *The Easy Yoke.* Colorado Springs: NavPress, 1995.

4. What do you do to experience rest and renewal? Do these activities deliver real rest, or do they actually drain you even more?

5. What is the difference between (1) taking some time off from school or work and (2) discovering a whole new way of bearing responsibilities?

6. Living overloaded lives means that we fail to acknowledge our limits. What keeps you from acknowledging your limits?

7. What is your best advice for people who have a hard time saying no to more responsibilities and commitments?

36 Life Essentials

BELIEVING
Authority of the Bible
Triune God
Great and Good God
Humanity
➤ **Satan and Sin**
Jesus Christ
Salvation
Holy Spirit
The Church
Transformation
Mission
The End

BEHAVING
Studying the Bible
Fellowshiping
Worshiping
Seeking the Kingdom
Waging Spiritual War
Following
Trusting and Acting
Walking by the Spirit
Serving
Praying
Engaging the World
Persevering

BECOMING
Truth
Love
Purity
Rest
Freedom
New Identity in Christ
Assurance
Fruit of the Spirit
Humility
Peace
Compassion
Hope

Not the Way It's Supposed to Be

Satan and Sin

Once, when I was in college, a senior adult from our church invited me and several of my friends to eat Sunday dinner at her house. This godly matriarch of our country congregation also happened to be the personification of Southern sophistication. When we arrived at her home, the formal dining-room table was set with china, silver, and crystal. We could see the roast and gravy, the mashed potatoes supporting tiny lakes of butter, the carefully seasoned garden vegetables, and the homemade rolls. We guessed that there had to be a bodacious dessert hiding close by. Soon after we started devouring the delicious meal, I used a small silver spoon to scoop white powder from a crystal cube into my iced tea. "Several scoops of sugar ought to do it," I reasoned. When I took a big drink of my "sweet" tea, it didn't taste like sweet tea. It didn't even taste like unsweetened tea; it tasted like the ocean. Something had gone terribly wrong. To make a long story short, I had liberally salted my iced tea.

The story of Scripture takes a similar, but much more serious turn in Genesis 3. As you read the first two chapters of Genesis, you can't help but notice the repeated phrase, "God saw that it was good." All is well with God's creation. God even gives Eve to Adam as the perfect partner, and together they experience an intimate relationship with God and harmony with his creation. Then something goes terribly wrong, something much worse than pouring salt into a glass of iced tea. In Genesis 3 the background music changes as the deceiver crawls onto the scene and tempts Eve and Adam to take matters into their own hands (sin). They believe the lies of the serpent and act upon them. The results of their sin are disastrous, for both them and their descendants. We continue to suffer the consequences even today.

The Shattering of Shalom

The story of Scripture begins with our great and good God creating human beings in his image. Our triune God is the perfect community and created us to experience that life-giving community. A good biblical word for God's original plan for wholeness, delight, and abundance is the Hebrew word *shalom* ("peace"). This word refers to the "way things ought to be" as God, humans, and all creation live together in a perfect world.

The story takes a dark and dreadful turn in Genesis 3, however, when Satan and sin spoil God's good creation. More than anything, sin is the purposeful breaking of shalom. God hates sin "because it interferes with the way things are supposed to be" (Plantinga, *Not the Way It's Supposed to Be*, 14). As much as we would like to ignore this part of the story, we must face it in order to see how God wants to bring about a happy ending to the story by restoring the shalom he originally intended.

A Closer Look—Genesis 3:1–7

SCRIPTURE NOTES

[1]Now the serpent was more crafty than any of the wild animals

the LORD God had made. He said to the woman, "Did God

really say, 'You must not eat from any tree in the garden'?"

Although the Genesis story never specifically identifies the serpent as Satan or the Devil, this is the clear teaching of the New Testament:

> You belong to your father, the devil, and you want to carry out your father's desire. He was a murderer from the beginning, not holding to the truth, for there is no truth in him. When he lies, he speaks his native language, for he is a liar and the father of lies. (John 8:44)

> The great dragon was hurled down—that ancient serpent called the devil, or Satan, who leads the whole world astray. (Rev. 12:9)

> He seized the dragon, that ancient serpent, who is the devil, or Satan, and bound him for a thousand years. (Rev. 20:2)

1. Satan (meaning "adversary" or "opponent") is the chief evil spirit in a kingdom of evil. Look up the following verses, and write down what they say about Satan and his work.

   • Matthew 4:1–11

   • Mark 4:13–20

What Exactly Is Sin?

There are more than thirty words in the New Testament alone that convey the idea of sin. One reliable theologian defines sin as "any act, attitude, or disposition which fails to completely fulfill or measure up to the standards of God's righteousness. It may involve an actual transgression of God's law or failure to live up to his norms" (Erickson, *Concise Dictionary*, 152).

When we disobey or rebel, we sin. When we fall short of God's standard, we sin. When we place something other than God in God's place, we sin. When we listen to impressions rather than God's instructions, we sin. When we pervert God's good gifts into something self-serving, we sin. When we refuse to admit that we are needy creatures, we sin. We have all sinned and failed to live up to God's glorious design. And sin pays a wage—death.

- Mark 5:1–20

- John 12:30–32

- 2 Corinthians 4:4

- 2 Corinthians 11:14

- Ephesians 4:27

- Ephesians 6:11

- Hebrews 2:14–15

- James 4:7

- 1 Peter 5:8

- 1 John 3:8–10

- Revelation 12:7–9

2. In Genesis 3 Satan's strategy to deceive Eve begins with a loaded question. What is the deceiver trying to accomplish by starting the temptation in this way? What do you see imbedded in the serpent's question?

[2]The woman said to the serpent, "We may eat fruit from the trees in the garden, [3]but God did say, 'You must not eat fruit from the tree that is in the middle of the garden, and you must not touch it, or you will die.'"

BELIEVING 2—*Satan and Sin*

3. When Eve corrects the serpent, she actually goes too far and puts words in God's mouth. Carefully compare God's instructions in Genesis 2:16–17 with Eve's paraphrase in 3:2–3. What does Eve add?

SCRIPTURE NOTES

4"You will not surely die," the serpent said to the woman. 5"For

God knows that when you eat of it your eyes will be opened,

and you will be like God, knowing good and evil."

4. These verses reveal the next phase in the serpent's strategy. What does this involve?

SCRIPTURE NOTES

6When the woman saw that the fruit of the tree was good for

food and pleasing to the eye, and also desirable for gaining

wisdom, she took some and ate it. She also gave some to her

husband, who was with her, and he ate it.

5. Look at the verbs in verse 6 and identify the specific steps to sin.

⁷Then the eyes of both of them were opened, and they realized they were naked; so they sewed fig leaves together and made coverings for themselves.

Take and Eat

She took . . . and ate—so simple the act, so hard its undoing. God will taste poverty and death before "take and eat" become verbs of salvation.

—Derek Kidner, *Genesis*, 68

6. We have now moved from temptation to sin to consequences. Read the rest of Genesis 3 and record how sin affects relationships:

• Effects on the sinner's relationship with God

• Effects on the sinner

• Effects on the sinner's relationships with other humans

Evil in Disguise

Satan must appeal to our God-given appetite for goodness in order to win his way. . . . To prevail, evil must leech not only power and intelligence from goodness but also its credibility. From counterfeit money to phony airliner parts to the trustworthy look on the face of a con artist, evil appears in disguise. Hence its treacherousness. Hence the need for the Holy Spirit's gift of discernment. Hence the sheer difficulty, at times, of distinguishing what is good from what is evil.

—Cornelius Plantinga,
Not the Way It's Supposed to Be, 98

Crossing the Bridge

In order to cross the bridge from the ancient world to our world, we need to identify timeless theological truths that God is trying to teach us. There are a few principles listed below. What other theological principles do you see in Genesis 3:1–7?

• The tempter does not give up easily. Even after Eve's initial resistance, he keeps on pressuring her to sin.

• The tempter twists and distorts God's Word.

•

•

•

•

So What?

1. In the sinless garden environment, Adam and Eve still have God-given limits (2:16–17). What does that arrangement say about the nature of true freedom?

2. Satan's strategy to tempt human beings is subtle, deceitful, and complex. What aspect of that ancient strategy do you struggle with the most (e.g., not knowing what God really said, doubting God's motives)?

Cross-References
See the earlier references to Satan along with the following references to sin: Ps. 51; Matt. 4:1–11; Rom. 1–3; 5:6–8; 6:23; 8:1–4; 2 Cor. 11:14–15; Eph. 2:1–6; James 1:13–15; 4:17; 1 John 1:8–10; 2:15–17

3. How does understanding Satan's strategy help us better understand the nature of sin?

For Deeper Study
Lewis, C. S. *The Screwtape Letters.* New York: Macmillan, 1961.
Plantinga, Cornelius. *Not the Way It's Supposed to Be: A Breviary of Sin.* Grand Rapids: Eerdmans, 1995.
Walton, John H. *Genesis.* NIV Application Commentary. Grand Rapids: Zondervan, 2001.

4. C. S. Lewis once wrote, "There are two equal and opposite errors into which our [human] race can fall about the devils. One is to disbelieve in their existence. The other is to believe, and to feel an excessive and unhealthy interest in them. They themselves are equally pleased by both errors" (*Screwtape Letters*, ix). Do you tend toward one extreme or the other? What do you need in order to be more discerning?

5. When is it most difficult to trust that God wants what is best for you?

6. How do you see people acting as if they were God? What is your greatest struggle in this area?

36 Life Essentials

BELIEVING
Authority of the Bible
Triune God
Great and Good God
Humanity
Satan and Sin
Jesus Christ
Salvation
Holy Spirit
The Church
Transformation
Mission
The End

BEHAVING
Studying the Bible
Fellowshiping
Worshiping
Seeking the Kingdom
➤ **Waging Spiritual War**
Following
Trusting and Acting
Walking by the Spirit
Serving
Praying
Engaging the World
Persevering

BECOMING
Truth
Love
Purity
Rest
Freedom
New Identity in Christ
Assurance
Fruit of the Spirit
Humility
Peace
Compassion
Hope

Our Struggle Is Not Against Flesh and Blood

Waging Spiritual War

We don't live in a perfect world. We have enemies. Satan entices us to look for life apart from God, and sometimes we take him up on the offer. The consequences can be deadly. The apostle Peter tells us that our "enemy the devil prowls around like a roaring lion looking for someone to devour" (1 Peter 5:8). We also battle our own sinful tendency to walk away from God, to go our own way. We read in Romans that "all have sinned and fall short of the glory of God" (3:23), and we can relate. Yes, we have enemies, but we also have a Savior who has conquered those enemies. In Jesus' showdown with Satan at the beginning of our Lord's public ministry, he doesn't retreat in ignorance or cower in fear. Instead Jesus wins the victory in the Judean wilderness and advances the kingdom of God. In Behaving 2, we look to Jesus' example of how to wage spiritual war. Get ready to put on your armor!

In his profoundly insightful and inspiring book, *The Jesus I Never Knew*, Philip Yancey observes how Jesus' temptation in the wilderness reveals the difference between how God works and how Satan works and teaches us that goodness cannot be imposed from the outside; it must grow from the inside out.

The Temptation in the desert reveals a profound difference between God's power and Satan's power. Satan has the power to coerce, to dazzle, to force obedience, to destroy. Humans have learned much from that power, and governments draw deeply from its reservoir. With a bullwhip or a billy club or an AK-47, human beings can force other human beings to do just about anything they want. . . . Satan's power is external and coercive.

God's power, in contrast, is internal and noncoercive. . . . Such power may seem at times like weakness. In its commitment to transform gently from the inside out and in its relentless dependence on human choice, God's power may resemble a kind of abdication. As every parent and every lover knows, love can be rendered powerless if the beloved chooses to spurn it. . . .

Although power can force obedience, only love can summon a response of love, which is the one thing God wants from us and the reason he created us. . . . Love has its own power, the only power ultimately capable of conquering the human heart. (pages 76–78)

Part of waging spiritual war includes understanding your enemy. Satan tries to coerce, to force, to overpower, but how? What is his strategy? Adam and Eve's experience in the garden (Gen. 3) and Jesus' battle in the desert (Matt. 4) answer that question.

A Closer Look—Matthew 4:1–11

Take a moment and read Matthew 3:13–4:17. Notice anything in these surrounding paragraphs that might help you understand 4:1–11. For example, you might notice that Jesus had just heard his Father say, "This is My Son" (3:17) before going into the desert to hear Satan say, "If [Since] you are the Son . . ." This tells us that Satan is not really doubting that Jesus is the Son of God. Rather, he is tempting Jesus to use his divine power in selfish ways.

1. What else do you see in the surrounding context of 3:13–17 and 4:12–17?

Now look carefully at the passage itself. Note repeated words or phrases, commands, contrasts, purpose statements, time and place references, and so on. Mark up the passage below and make comments in the margins.

¹Then Jesus was led by the Spirit into the desert to be tempted

by the devil. ²After fasting forty days and forty nights, he was

hungry. ³The tempter came to him and said, "If you are the Son

THE POWER OF WORDS

"it is written"—Each time Jesus answers Satan's temptation, he answers with "it is written" followed by a quotation from his Bible, the Old Testament. All three times Jesus quotes from Deuteronomy 6–8. This part of Deuteronomy records Moses' sermons to the people of Israel just before they crossed the Jordan River into the Promised Land. Moses was challenging Israel to be faithful!

Ironically, Jesus had just been baptized in the same Jordan River and was about to begin his public ministry. Jesus, the obedient Son, came to do what the disobedient children of Israel had failed to do. When tempted to do the right thing at the wrong time, or to test God rather than trust him, or to take a shortcut to his crown, Jesus responds by citing God's Word in context.

A Mighty Fortress
And though this world, with devils filled,
Should threaten to undo us,
We will not fear, for God hath willed
His truth to triumph through us.
The Prince of Darkness grim,
We tremble not for him;
His rage we can endure,
For lo, his doom is sure,
One little word shall fell him.
—Martin Luther,
"A Mighty Fortress Is Our God"

SCRIPTURE NOTES

of God, tell these stones to become bread." ⁴Jesus answered, "It is written: 'Man does not live on bread alone, but on every word that comes from the mouth of God.'" ⁵Then the devil took him to the holy city and had him stand on the highest point of the temple. ⁶"If you are the Son of God," he said, "throw yourself down. For it is written: 'He will command his angels concerning you, and they will lift you up in their hands, so that you will not strike your foot against a stone.'" ⁷Jesus answered him, "It is also written: 'Do not put the Lord your God to the test.'" ⁸Again, the devil took him to a very high mountain and showed him all the kingdoms of the world and their splendor. ⁹"All this I will give you," he said, "if you will bow down and worship me." ¹⁰Jesus said to him, "Away from me, Satan! For it is written: 'Worship the Lord your God, and serve him only.'"

¹¹Then the devil left him, and angels came and attended him.

A Desperate Housewife
Read Genesis 39 and put yourself in Joseph's place. Reflect on the things that set him up for temptation, on his response, on the cost of resisting, and so on. What is the main thing you take away from this interesting story about waging spiritual battle?

2. Think a moment about the similarities between Satan's strategy in tempting Adam and Eve (Gen. 3:1–7) and his strategy in tempting Jesus (Matt. 4:1–11). Make a list of the tempter's strategies that are common to both situations.

- Satan raises doubts about God's Word.
- Satan appeals to their physical desires.
-
-
-
-
-
-
-
-

Look carefully at your list since it offers a significant clue about what to expect from the tempter in your own life. His strategy doesn't change.

Crossing the Bridge

In order to cross the bridge from the ancient world to our world, we need to identify timeless theological truths that God is trying to teach us. There are a few principles listed below. What other theological principles do you see in Matthew 4:1–11?

- The same situation can be experienced by the same person as both a test from God and a temptation from Satan. Jesus was "led *by the Spirit* into the desert to be tempted *by the devil.*"

- The essence of temptation is to twist something good into something evil. Usually a temptation is not something inherently evil, but something good used for evil purposes. One very important aspect of waging spiritual war is to know the true purpose, God's purpose, for things we encounter in life.

-

-

-

-

-

So What?

1. When Satan tempts Jesus, he appeals to several universal human desires. What are they? How does Satan appeal to those same desires when tempting you?

Be strong with the Lord's mighty power. Put on all of God's armor so that you will be able to stand firm against all strategies and tricks of the Devil. For we are not fighting against people made of flesh and blood, but against the evil rulers and authorities of the unseen world, against those mighty powers of darkness who rule this world, and against wicked spirits in the heavenly realms. Use every piece of God's armor to resist the enemy in the time of evil, so that after the battle you will still be standing firm. Stand your ground, putting on the sturdy belt of truth and the body armor of God's righteousness. For shoes, put on the peace that comes from the Good News, so that you will be fully prepared. In every battle you will need faith as your shield to stop the fiery arrows aimed at you by Satan. Put on salvation as your helmet, and take the sword of the Spirit, which is the word of God. Pray at all times and on every occasion in the power of the Holy Spirit. Stay alert and be persistent in your prayers for all Christians everywhere.

—Ephesians 6:10–18 NLT

Anything but Action

In Lewis's Screwtape Letters *everything is turned upside down as an older devil, Screwtape, gives advice to a novice demon, Wormwood, about how to tempt a young man.*

The great thing is to prevent his doing anything. As long as he does not convert it into action, it does not matter how much he thinks about his new repentance. Let the little brute wallow in it. Let him . . . write a book about it; . . . Let him do anything but act. No amount of piety in his imagination and affections will harm us if we can keep it out of his will. . . . The more often he feels without acting, the less he will be able ever to act, and, in the long run, the less he will be able to feel.

—C. S. Lewis,
Screwtape Letters, 66–67

Cross-References
Gen. 39; 1 Cor. 10:13; Eph. 6:10–20; Heb. 4:15–16; James 4:1–10

For Deeper Study
Arnold, Clinton. *Three Crucial Questions About Spiritual Warfare.* Grand Rapids: Baker, 1997.
Fape, Michael O. *Powers in Encounter with Power.* Scotland: Christian Focus, 2003.
Wilkins, Michael J. *Matthew.* NIV Application Commentary. Grand Rapids: Zondervan, 2004.
Wright, Nigel Goring. *A Theology of the Dark Side: Putting the Power of Evil in Its Place.* Downers Grove, IL: InterVarsity Press, 2003.

2. Since evil is usually a perverting and twisting of something good, temptation will often relate to some God-given need in our lives. What legitimate needs do you have that are not being met? How are you tempted to meet those needs in illegitimate ways?

3. One of Jesus' weapons for waging spiritual war is using Scripture. What other weapons do you see Jesus using in Matthew 4:1–11?

4. Read Ephesians 6:10–18 in the sidebar on page 43. What role should prayer play in waging spiritual war?

5. When are you most vulnerable to spiritual attack?

6. Summarize the main thing you have learned in Behaving 2 about waging spiritual war.

7. As you think about a temptation you are now facing in your life, how can you apply what you have learned to your particular situation?

Free at Last, Free at Last

Freedom

Our belief that Satan and sin are dangerous enemies leads to the practice of waging spiritual warfare. We turned to Jesus' temptations in the desert to see how he countered the lies and deception of the Evil One. Very simply, he defeated Satan by trusting his Father, relying upon the truth of the Scriptures, and walking in obedience. The character quality that results from a belief in the reality of spiritual enemies and the habit of waging war against them is freedom—the topic of Becoming 2.

On August 28, 1963, Martin Luther King Jr. stood at a podium at the Lincoln Memorial in Washington DC and delivered his famous "I Have a Dream" speech. One hundred years earlier Abraham Lincoln had signed the Emancipation Proclamation, a "momentous decree" King said, that "came as a beacon light of hope to millions of Negro slaves, . . . a joyous daybreak to the end of the long night of their captivity." King's message culminates with the following words:

And when this happens, when we allow freedom to ring, when we let it ring from every village and every hamlet, from every state and every city, we will be able to speed up that day when *all* of God's children, black men and white men, Jews and Gentiles, Protestants and Catholics, will be able to join hands and sing in the words of the old Negro spiritual,

"Free at last, free at last.
Thank God Almighty, we are free at last."

King was a Baptist minister whose deep Christian faith fueled his passion for leading the civil rights movement in the turbulent America of the 1960s. As a result of his courageous commitment to fight for the social

36 Life Essentials

BELIEVING
Authority of the Bible
Triune God
Great and Good God
Humanity
Satan and Sin
Jesus Christ
Salvation
Holy Spirit
The Church
Transformation
Mission
The End

BEHAVING
Studying the Bible
Fellowshiping
Worshiping
Seeking the Kingdom
Waging Spiritual War
Following
Trusting and Acting
Walking by the Spirit
Serving
Praying
Engaging the World
Persevering

BECOMING
Truth
Love
Purity
Rest
➤ **Freedom**
New Identity in Christ
Assurance
Fruit of the Spirit
Humility
Peace
Compassion
Hope

implications of the gospel of Jesus Christ, Martin Luther King Jr. was assassinated April 4, 1968, on the balcony outside his Memphis hotel room.

The God revealed in Scripture is a God of deliverance. The Old Testament offers many examples of God setting people free. The greatest example, of course, is the exodus, when God delivered his people from slavery in Egypt. The famous Ten Commandments of Exodus 20 begin with these words—"I am the LORD your God, who brought you out of Egypt, out of the land of slavery" (v. 2). The Old Testament also looks forward to a time when God would make a new covenant with his people and write his law on their hearts (Jer. 31:33). He would set them free from the inside out through the work of his Spirit. Leading his people out of slavery in Egypt was a preview of the ultimate work of rescue and deliverance accomplished by Jesus Christ. At the cross God condemned the power of sin so that all who respond to Jesus are no longer condemned but set free to live—really live!

A Closer Look—Romans 8:1–4

1. Read Romans 7. What is Paul's dilemma in this chapter?

Now look at Romans 8:1–4 below. Read the passage carefully, marking important words, purpose statements, prepositions, explanations, conjunctions, and so on. In addition, make comments, show connections, or ask questions in the margins.

SCRIPTURE NOTES

¹Therefore, there is now no condemnation for those who are in Christ Jesus, ²because through Christ Jesus the law of the Spirit of life set me free from the law of sin and death. ³For what the law was powerless to do in that it was weakened by the sinful nature, God did by sending his own Son in the likeness of sinful man to be a sin offering. And so he condemned sin in sinful man, ⁴in order that the righteous requirements of the law might be fully met in us, who do not live according to the sinful nature but according to the Spirit.

2. Why is there no condemnation for us? What is the absolute requirement to receive the pardon? What else does this text say about condemnation?

3. If God's law is good, why is it powerless to set us free?

4. What are the three "laws" in this text, and how do they relate to each other?

5. When it says in verse 3 that "God did" something, what did God actually do?

6. How can we meet the demands and standards of God's perfect law?

Crossing the Bridge

This passage is loaded with theological truths that can make a big difference in our lives. For example, rules (law) are good, but they have no power to set us free from sin. Rules can only show us what is right and wrong; they cannot help us do what is right or avoid what is wrong. The Law points out the problem, but it is powerless to supply a solution. What other theological principles do you see in Romans 8:1–4?

-
-
-

"condemnation"—The underlying Greek word occurs only in Romans 5:16 and 18 and here in 8:1 in the New Testament. This legal term refers to judgment against someone and the resulting penalty. When one is condemned spiritually, that person is separated from God for eternity. Since God condemned sin through the death of Jesus, those who are joined to Christ are removed from condemnation forever. Only the Judge can condemn, and he has done everything that is required to deliver us from condemnation. When we receive Christ, we receive God's pardon from condemnation. Now there is NO condemnation!

"law of the Spirit of life"—This expression denotes the liberating power of the Holy Spirit exerted through the life, death, and resurrection of Jesus Christ. The Spirit sets us free from the power of sin and the spiritual death that results from sin.

"sinful nature"—Sometimes translated "flesh," this word can refer to the physical body (1 Cor. 6:16) or to human beings in general (Rom. 3:20). The word is used here, however, to describe the condition or situation of people outside of Jesus Christ (i.e., spiritual bondage). As Christians we are no longer in this condition, and we should not live as if we are.

Why We Fight

In one of the last episodes of the World War II series *Band of Brothers*, Easy Company scouts the area surrounding a German town they have recently occupied. The American soldiers are totally unprepared for what they discover. Outside of town they stumble onto a prison camp for Polish Jews. The camp is filled with disease and death. Battle-hardened soldiers stare in disbelief as they behold the work of Satan and sin. No wonder they labeled this particular episode, "Why We Fight." In the same way, Jesus came to destroy the Devil's work (1 John 3:8) and set people free.

Source of Freedom

John 8:31–59 records an intense conversation between Jesus and the Jewish religious leaders. Notice how much he talks about slavery and freedom in verses 31–36:

To the Jews who had believed him, Jesus said, "If you hold to my teaching, you are really my disciples. Then you will know the truth, and the truth will set you free." They answered him, "We are Abraham's descendants and have never been slaves of anyone. How can you say that we shall be set free?" Jesus replied, "I tell you the truth, everyone who sins is a slave to sin. Now a slave has no permanent place in the family, but a son belongs to it forever. So if the Son sets you free, you will be free indeed."

—John 8:31–36

Cross-References

Jer. 31:31–34; Ezek. 11:17–20; 36:24–27; Luke 4:18–19; John 3:18; 8:31–36; Rom. 5–8; 2 Cor. 3:17–18; Gal. 3–5; Eph. 2:1–5; Col. 1:13–14; Titus 3:3; Heb. 2:14–15; 10:17–23; 1 Peter 2:16; 2 Peter 2:19

For Deeper Study

Cloud, Henry, and John Townsend. *How People Grow.* Grand Rapids: Zondervan, 2001.

Fee, Gordon D. *God's Empowering Presence.* Peabody, MA: Hendrickson, 1994.

Moo, Douglas J. *Romans.* NIV Application Commentary. Grand Rapids: Zondervan, 2000.

So What?

1. If you are "in Christ," you are free from condemnation. God is for you, not against you! Do you ever catch yourself thinking that God still wants to condemn you now or plans to condemn you at the final judgment? If you are still expecting condemnation, what else could God do to convince you that you are free?

2. What is God's goal in setting us free from the law of sin and death?

3. Even Christians can sometimes become enslaved again when they choose to live according to the flesh instead of according to the Spirit. What things or people tend to enslave you these days?

4. What is one practical step you could take this week to live in freedom rather than bondage? How can your Christian community help you?

5. What has the Lord been saying to you through this last series: Belief About Satan and Sin → Behavior in Spiritual Warfare → Becoming Free?

The Word Became Flesh

Jesus Christ

36 Life Essentials

BELIEVING
Authority of the Bible
Triune God
Great and Good God
Humanity
Satan and Sin
➤ **Jesus Christ**
Salvation
Holy Spirit
The Church
Transformation
Mission
The End

BEHAVING
Studying the Bible
Fellowshiping
Worshiping
Seeking the Kingdom
Waging Spiritual War
Following
Trusting and Acting
Walking by the Spirit
Serving
Praying
Engaging the World
Persevering

BECOMING
Truth
Love
Purity
Rest
Freedom
New Identity in Christ
Assurance
Fruit of the Spirit
Humility
Peace
Compassion
Hope

The heart of the Christian faith is a person. In a real sense Christianity *is* Jesus Christ. Our faith in Jesus includes accepting his teachings, trusting his death on the cross for us, believing that God raised him from the dead, and looking forward to his future return. But our faith in Jesus all starts with recognizing who he is. The rescue story begins with God meeting us where we are. When God the Son became a human being, God came looking for us. The technical term for God becoming a man is *incarnation,* a word that means "being in flesh." Think for a second about why God had to become a human.

Sin caused a break in our relationship with God. Like Adam and Eve, we hid from God in our shame and fear. Yet because of God's great compassion, he came after us—not to condemn us, but to heal us and offer us a way home. God sent his Son to rescue us from Satan and sin and restore us to a right relationship with him.

> For God so loved the world that he gave his one and only Son, that whoever believes in him shall not perish but have eternal life. For God did not send his Son into the world to condemn the world, but to save the world through him. (John 3:16–17)

In order to rescue us, God the Son became a flesh-and-blood human being—Jesus of Nazareth. The Son has always existed and is completely equal to God the Father. He is the eternal Son of God (one person) who is at the same time fully God and fully man (two natures). John 1:14 puts it this way, "The Word became flesh." Philip Yancey learned more about God becoming a human being (incarnation) from, of all things, his pet fish.

> I learned about incarnation when I kept a salt-water aquarium. Management of a marine aquarium, I discovered, is no easy task. I had to run a portable chemical laboratory to monitor the nitrate levels and the ammonia content. I pumped in vitamins and antibodies and

sulfa drugs and enough enzymes to make a rock grow. I filtered the water through glass fibers and charcoal, and exposed it to ultraviolet light. You would think, in view of all the energy expended on their behalf, that my fish would at least be grateful. Not so. Every time my shadow loomed above the tank they dove for cover into the nearest shell. They showed me one "emotion" only: fear. Although I opened the lid and dropped in food on a regular schedule, three times a day, they responded to each visit as a sure sign of my designs to torture them. I could not convince them of my true concern.

To my fish I was deity. I was too large for them, my actions too incomprehensible. My acts of mercy they saw as cruelty; my attempts at healing they viewed as destruction. To change their perceptions, I began to see, would require a form of incarnation. I would have to become a fish and "speak" to them in a language they could understand.

A human being becoming a fish is nothing compared to God becoming a baby. And yet according to the Gospels that is what happened at Bethlehem. The God who created matter took shape within it, as an artist might become a spot on a painting or a playwright a character within his own play. God wrote a story, only using real characters, on the pages of real history. The Word became flesh. (*The Jesus I Never Knew*, 38–39)

The early Christians concluded that Jesus was completely divine and completely human. In the process they rejected these two defective explanations of the Incarnation:

- Adoptionism—The belief that God the Father adopted a man (Jesus) to be his Son. This took place at his baptism, and sometime later (probably at the cross), God abandoned the man Jesus.
- Docetism—The view that Jesus was a divine being who only pretended to be a real man. Jesus wasn't really human; he just appeared to be human. He was God putting on a human suit.

Both of these views were rejected because they fail to explain what the Gospels tell us, and because they leave us without a real savior. If Jesus was not both human and divine, he could not rescue us from Satan and sin. *If he was just a man*, he could not save us since he also would need someone to save him. *If he was not a man*, he would have no real connection to us as humans and wouldn't be able to die a real death for our sins.

To be able to reconnect us to God, Jesus had to be both divine and human. Since he is human, he can sympathize with us, experience what it means to be human, suffer, and die. Since he is divine, he can live a sinless life and his death on the cross can pay the just penalty for sin. God himself then provides the sacrifice that he requires.

BELIEVING 3—*Jesus Christ*

JESUS IS GOD	JESUS IS HUMAN
Claimed to be God (John 19:7)	Said he was a man (John 8:40)
Addressed as Lord (Acts 2:36)	Human ancestors (Matt. 1)
Eternal (John 8:58)	Had a real body (1 John 1:1)
One with Father (John 10:30)	Grew and developed (Luke 2)
Authority to forgive (Luke 5)	Became hungry, thirsty, and tired (John 4)
Performed miracles (Mark 4–5)	Was tempted (Matt. 4:1)
Recognized as Lord (Rom. 10:9)	Sinless human (Heb. 4:15)
Disciples saw as God (Matt. 20)	Sorrowful and troubled (Matt. 26:37)
Sinless (2 Cor. 5:21; 1 John 3:5)	Suffered and died (John 19)
Worshiped as God (Matt. 28)	
Crucified for claims (Mark 14–15)	
Raised from the dead (Luke 24)	

In *The Rescue*, the third workbook in the Experiencing God's Story series, we will discover more about Jesus' death and resurrection. For now, let's take a closer look at the Word becoming flesh as described in John 1.

A Closer Look—John 1:1–3, 14, 18

Begin by reading John 1:1–18 in your Bible. Then carefully study the passage below. Circle repeated words, identify lists, underline prepositional phrases, note characteristics of the Word, and so on. Jot down your observations in the margins.

¹In the beginning was the Word, and the Word was with God, and the Word was God. ²He was with God in the beginning. ³Through him all things were made; without him nothing was made that has been made. . . . ¹⁴The Word became flesh and made his dwelling among us. We have seen his glory, the glory of the One and Only, who came from the Father, full of grace and truth. . . . ¹⁸No one has ever seen God, but God the One and Only, who is at the Father's side, has made him known.

THE POWER OF WORDS

"made his dwelling"—During the wilderness wanderings of Israel, God made his presence known in a temporary tent called a tabernacle. God filled that tent with his presence and his glory. John 1:14 literally says the Word (Jesus) "tabernacled" or "pitched his tent" among us. God came to live among us in the person of Jesus Christ. The same word is used again in Revelation 21:3, where we are told that God will make his permanent home among his people in the new heaven and new earth.

"made him known"—No one has seen God the Father, but God the Son has revealed, or explained, him. This word literally means "to exegete," or lead out. Jesus Christ leads out, or makes known, the heart of the invisible God. Only Jesus Christ, who has the very nature of God, can really show us what the Father is like. If you want to know what God is like, look at Jesus.

SCRIPTURE NOTES

The Greek word for **fish** is ΙΧΘΥΣ (*Ichthus*). It was used by early Christians as an acronym that spoke of Jesus and his mission.

Ι — Jesus

Χ — Christ

Θ — God's

Υ — Son

Σ — Savior

What's in a Name?

"Jesus"—The angel told Joseph, "You are to give him the name Jesus, because he will save his people from their sins" (Matt. 1:21). The name "Jesus" literally means "The Lord saves." Jesus came to rescue or save us from Satan and sin.

"Christ"—This is not Jesus' last name but a title, "the Christ." The term "Christ" (Greek) is equivalent to "Messiah" (Hebrew), or "anointed one." In the Old Testament the person anointed with oil was singled out by God as being very important and having a special mission. Over time, the term *Christ* came to mean something more like "deliverer" or "rescuer." Again, Jesus is the one who will deliver his people from their enemies.

Crossing the Bridge

From your careful study of the verses on page 95, what messages does God seem to be communicating through this text? Write out present-tense statements that (a) reflect what the text says and means and (b) apply equally to the ancient audience and the contemporary audience. Sometimes biblical principles relate to who God is rather than what we are supposed to do.

- Jesus Christ is fully God and existed as God before time began ("in the beginning," cf. Gen. 1:1).

- Jesus Christ was involved in creation ("through him all things were made").

-

-

-

So What?

1. Jesus himself is a picture of God. As you think about what Jesus said and did, what is the most meaningful aspect of that portrait for you? In other words, in what ways does reading about Jesus help you understand God?

2. Why did Jesus have to be 100 percent God and 100 percent man in order to rescue us from Satan and sin?

3. Which is more difficult for you to believe—that Jesus is fully divine or fully human? Why?

4. What would you say is the most comforting element of Jesus being a real human being—that he was tempted, that he suffered, or what?

5. What are some ways that we can live "incarnational" lives as believers?

Cross-References
Matt. 1:23; Luke 1:35; John 10:30–38; Rom. 8:3; 9:5; Gal. 4:4–5; Phil. 2:5–11; Col. 1:15, 19; 2:2–9; Titus 2:13; Heb. 1:1–3; 2:14; 1 John 1:1–4; 4:2; 5:20; Rev. 1:5–6; 5:12–13

For Deeper Study
Bock, Darrell L. *Jesus According to Scripture.* Grand Rapids: Baker, 2002.
Erickson, Millard J. *The Word Became Flesh: A Contemporary Incarnational Christology.* Grand Rapids: Baker, 1991.
McGrath, Alister E. *I Believe.* Downers Grove, IL: InterVarsity Press, 1997.
Morris, Leon. *The Gospel According to John.* Rev. ed. New International Commentary on the New Testament. Grand Rapids: Eerdmans, 1995.

36 Life Essentials

BELIEVING
Authority of the Bible
Triune God
Great and Good God
Humanity
Satan and Sin
Jesus Christ
Salvation
Holy Spirit
The Church
Transformation
Mission
The End

BEHAVING
Studying the Bible
Fellowshiping
Worshiping
Seeking the Kingdom
Waging Spiritual War
➤ **Following**
Trusting and Acting
Walking by the Spirit
Serving
Praying
Engaging the World
Persevering

BECOMING
Truth
Love
Purity
Rest
Freedom
New Identity in Christ
Assurance
Fruit of the Spirit
Humility
Peace
Compassion
Hope

The Cost of Discipleship

Following

Dietrich Bonhoeffer, a German pastor during the second World War, was eventually hanged by the Nazis for his resistance against that evil regime. In his book, *The Cost of Discipleship,* Bonhoeffer wrote, "The cross is laid on every Christian. . . . When Christ calls a man, He bids him come and die" (page 99). In Believing 3 we focused on our belief that God the Son became a human being in order to rescue us, that he lived a sinless life, died on the cross as our substitute, and was raised from the dead. Now we will see that the same Jesus who gave his all for us demands that we give our all to him. His gift to us is also his demand of us. Grace is free, but it is not cheap. In this study we turn our attention to the habit of choosing to follow Jesus in every area of life.

Take a moment and read Mark 8:27–9:1, the context for our focal passage. You will notice that Simon Peter answers Jesus' question correctly (8:29— "You are the Christ") only to be rebuked a few minutes later (8:33—"Get behind me, Satan!"). Imagine for a moment that you are Simon Peter and that you are making your journal entry at the end of this very confusing day. What would you write?

As Jesus moves closer to dying on the cross, he begins to teach his followers about the kind of Rescuer (Messiah, or Christ) he came to be. The disciples, like other Jewish people of Jesus' day, expected the Messiah to liberate them from Roman rule. They expected a political or military Messiah. No doubt, Jesus shocks them with the news that he will suffer and die in Jerusalem. The problem is that they cannot conceive of a "crucified messiah." According to their way of thinking, deliverers don't get themselves crucified and conquering kings don't go down in defeat.

Surprisingly, when Jesus tells them about his own impending rejection and death, he adds a few sentences about a cross they would have to carry. To be sure, only Jesus could carry his cross to Calvary to die for the sins of humanity, but he's not the only one who must carry a cross.

A Closer Look—Mark 8:34–38

Carefully study the following passage by answering the standard story questions—Who? What? When? Where? Why? and How? Write your answers and observations below.

THE POWER OF WORDS

"deny himself"—This does not refer to denying something to ourselves but to denying ourselves the right to control life. Self-denial means saying "no" to selfish desires and ambitions so that we may say "yes" to Jesus.

"take up his cross"—This is not talking about the burdens that all humans bear (e.g., an illness or a difficult relative) but about our willingness to face rejection and ridicule because we follow Jesus.

SCRIPTURE NOTES

³⁴Then he called the crowd to him along with his disciples and said: "If anyone would come after me, he must deny himself and take up his cross and follow me. ³⁵For whoever wants to save his life will lose it, but whoever loses his life for me and for the gospel will save it. ³⁶What good is it for a man to gain the whole world, yet forfeit his soul? ³⁷Or what can a man give in exchange for his soul? ³⁸If anyone is ashamed of me and my words in this adulterous and sinful generation, the Son of Man will be ashamed of him when he comes in his Father's glory with the holy angels."

Crossing the Bridge

From your careful study of Mark 8:34–38, you can begin to see what God is trying to say through this text. In the space provided, write out several principles that capture the timeless truths God is communicating through these verses.

- People must choose to follow Jesus Christ. He will not force them to follow.

- The requirements are the same for everyone who chooses to follow Christ—deny self, take up the cross, and follow.

Count the Cost

That is why He warned people to "count the cost" before becoming Christians. "Make no mistake," He says, "if you let Me, I will make you perfect. The moment you put yourself in My hands, that is what you are in for. Nothing less, or other, than that. You have free will, and if you choose, you can push Me away. But if you do not push Me away, understand that I am going to see this job through. Whatever suffering it may cost you in your earthly life, . . . I will never rest, nor let you rest, until you are literally perfect—until my Father can say without reservation that He is well pleased with you, . . . This I can do and will do. But I will not do anything less."

—C. S. Lewis, *Mere Christianity*, 158

•

•

•

A *disciple* is a committed follower of a teacher or leader. The Pharisees had disciples (Matt. 22:15–16; Mark 2:18), as did John the Baptist (Mark 2:18; John 1:35; 3:25). If you study the New Testament thoroughly, you will discover what Michael Wilkins calls the nonnegotiables of biblical discipleship (*In His Image*, 61):

- It is grounded in a personal, costly relationship with Jesus.
- It results in a new identity in Jesus.
- It is guided by God's Word.
- It is empowered by the Holy Spirit.
- It is developed through a whole-life process.
- It is practiced in communities of faith.
- It is carried out in our everyday world.

Under "Cross-References" you will find a list of verses that relate to the topic of discipleship. Look up each of those texts and jot down your insights about the costs and blessings of following Jesus.

COSTS	BLESSINGS

The Shape of Self-Denial

Every day we must open ourselves up to God's initiatives and control. Self-denial takes shape in many ways. For some, it may mean leaving job and family as the disciples have done. For the proud, it means renouncing the desire for status and honor. For the greedy, it means renouncing an appetite for wealth. The complacent will have to renounce the love of ease. The fainthearted will have to abandon the craving for security. The violent will have to repudiate the desire for revenge. On it goes.

—David Garland, *Mark*, 333

So What?

1. Select one of the principles that you wrote earlier. How do you need to think differently or live differently in order to experience that truth more consistently in your life?

2. What is the most difficult aspect of "self" for you to deny?

3. List some specific costs of following Jesus in these areas of your life:

- family

- work or school

- relationships

- leisure time

- money

- eating habits

- attitudes

-

-

4. How do we know when rejection by others is caused by bearing the cross of genuine discipleship or when the ridicule stems from our own obnoxious and foolish ways?

5. In light of the context, what does Mark 8:36 mean for Peter and the other disciples? Have you ever had an expectation about how the Christian life should work that was either not fulfilled or was fulfilled in a different way?

Carrying a Rugged Cross

Jesus has many lovers of his heavenly kingdom these days, but few of them carry his cross. He has many who desire comfort, few who desire affliction. He has many friends to share his meals, but few to share his fasts. Everyone is eager to rejoice with him, but few are willing to endure anything for him. Many follow Jesus up to the breaking of bread, but few as far as drinking from the chalice of his passion. Many love Jesus as long as no difficulties touch them. Many praise and bless him as long as they receive comfort from him.

—Thomas à Kempis,
Imitation of Christ, 2.11

Cross-References

Matt. 7:24–27; 10:37–39; 11:29–30; 16:13–28; Mark 3:31–35; 10:29–31; Luke 6:22–23; 9:22–27, 59–62; 14:25–33; John 8:31–32; 14:21; 15:11, 21–22; 16:33; 20:19

For Deeper Study

Bonhoeffer, Dietrich. *The Cost of Discipleship.* New York: Macmillan, 1963.
Garland, David E. *Mark.* NIV Application Commentary. Grand Rapids: Zondervan, 1996.
Ogden, Greg. *Transforming Discipleship: Making Disciples a Few at a Time.* Downers Grove, IL: InterVarsity Press, 2003.

36 Life Essentials

BELIEVING
Authority of the Bible
Triune God
Great and Good God
Humanity
Satan and Sin
Jesus Christ
Salvation
Holy Spirit
The Church
Transformation
Mission
The End

BEHAVING
Studying the Bible
Fellowshiping
Worshiping
Seeking the Kingdom
Waging Spiritual War
Following
Trusting and Acting
Walking by the Spirit
Serving
Praying
Engaging the World
Persevering

BECOMING
Truth
Love
Purity
Rest
Freedom
➤ **New Identity in Christ**
Assurance
Fruit of the Spirit
Humility
Peace
Compassion
Hope

Out with the Old, In with the New

New Identity in Christ

God came to us in Jesus Christ. "The Word became flesh." He entered our world so that we might enter his world and experience the perfect love and fellowship that comes only from the triune God. Wow! Jesus is God incarnate, fully God and fully man. He came to us in order to rescue us from Satan and sin and give us real life. He came to give his all—yet the one who gave his all for us also demands our all. He calls us to deny ourselves, take up our cross, and follow him. Following Christ is costly and affects the very core of who we are. Christ followers take on a whole new identity. We become brand-new people. As the apostle Paul says, "If anyone is in Christ, he is a new creation; the old has gone, the new has come!" (2 Cor. 5:17). Our new identity in Christ is the subject of Becoming 3.

Have you ever failed God? It's not a pleasant thought, but sometimes we learn as much (or more) from our failures as we do from our successes. That is the case with a man we read about in the New Testament, a man who boasted far beyond his ability to be faithful. (Not that we've ever done that!) You'll recall that it was Simon Peter who rebuked Jesus when the Lord told his disciples that he had to go to Jerusalem to suffer and die (Mark 8:31–32). Peter couldn't conceive of a savior or rescuer who would get himself killed. Jesus' response was blunt and uncompromising, "Get behind me, Satan!" he said. "You do not have in mind the things of God, but the things of men" (Mark 8:33). Jesus would win the victory over sin and Satan, but he would do it God's way—not by military might or by political scheming, but by sacrificing his own life on a cruel cross. He would take our punishment, so that we (the guilty sinners) might receive his pardon. God's way is victory through sacrifice.

Even after a harsh rebuke, Peter kept on walking the road of self-sufficiency. He continued to hold on to his own dreams and expectations about how God should behave more than what Jesus was revealing to him. The night before he died on the cross, Jesus ate a last supper with his disciples. That evening Peter again boasted about his ability to remain faithful even though all others might fail.

> Then Jesus told them, "This very night you will all fall away on account of me. . . . But after I have risen, I will go ahead of you into Galilee." Peter replied, *"Even if all fall away on account of you, I never will."* "I tell you the truth," Jesus answered, "this very night, before the rooster crows, you will disown me three times." But Peter declared, *"Even if I have to die with you, I will never disown you."* And all the other disciples said the same. (Matt. 26:31–35)

The next phase of the story is rather famous. Within hours after his boast, Peter denies Jesus three times. Jesus was right, of course, and he does go to Jerusalem to suffer and die on a cross. On the third day, Jesus is raised from the dead—God wins his way!

A Closer Look—John 21:15–23

What about Simon Peter? He had rebuked Jesus and received a rebuke in return. He had boasted naively that he would stay faithful, but he had failed miserably. Jesus had done things his way, and now Peter was lost and confused. Yet Jesus was not finished with Simon Peter. (Take a minute to read John 21:1–14.) After breakfast, Jesus and Peter have a brief but historic conversation (John 21:15–17) that consists of three questions, three answers, and three challenges or affirmations.

3 QUESTIONS from Jesus	3 ANSWERS from Peter	3 CHALLENGES from Jesus
"Simon son of John, do you truly love [agapē] me more than these?"	"Yes, Lord," he said, "you know that I love [phileō] you."	"Feed my lambs."
"Simon son of John, do you truly love [agapē] me?"	"Yes, Lord, you know that I love [phileō] you."	"Take care of my sheep."
"Simon son of John, do you love [phileō] me?"	"Lord, you know all things; you know that I love [phileō] you."	"Feed my sheep."

John Ortberg captures the significance of the event as Peter comes to grips with his new identity in Christ:

> Now it's just Jesus and Peter before a little fire, a charcoal fire. "Simon, son of John . . ." Jesus doesn't even use his old nickname, Peter. He uses his formal name, as if to say, "I won't presume that

"fire of burning coals"—Interestingly, there are only two places in the New Testament where this expression is used. First, in John 18:18 we are told that Peter is standing by a "charcoal fire" (NASB) warming himself when he denies Christ the first time. Second, we read in John 21:9 that Jesus cooks breakfast for the disciples over a "charcoal fire" (NASB). Isn't it just like Jesus to consider the sights and smells of denial when creating the setting for restoration?

"do you love me?"—Two verbs for love are used in the questions and answers in this passage—*agapē* and *phileō* (see the chart to the left). Some writers suggest that *agapē* refers to God's kind of love while *phileō* refers to human love. Since both verbs are used in the New Testament of the Father's love for the Son, this distinction does not really hold up. Word meanings always depend on the specific context rather than on a dictionary definition. Here in John 21, Jesus seems to use these verbs interchangeably to simply mean "love." He also uses different words for "know," "feed/take care," and "lambs/sheep." We shouldn't think that Peter finally brings Jesus down to his level when Jesus switches from *agapē* to *phileō* in the final question. The two words are used simply to keep things interesting. God enjoys variety.

you want the old intimate relationship. I won't presume you still want to wear the name I gave you."

"Simon, son of John, do you love me?" Now Jesus is the vulnerable one. Now Jesus is the Lover waiting to hear the response of the one he loves. "Yes, Lord," Peter answers, but he doesn't fully trust his ability to assess even his own heart. You know everything. You know. I understand Peter's answer: Lord you know. As best I can, I do love you. When I'm in my right mind, I do. I want to, better than I do now. I don't even know the whole truth about my heart. Lord, you know.

"Then feed my sheep," Jesus says. Love and teach and guard and guide and serve the little flock that means all the world to me. Get back in the game. Three times this is repeated, until Peter is hurt. Why does Jesus keep asking? . . .

The significance of the repetition is not in the synonyms but in the number of times the question is repeated. Three times. Peter does not know what we do, that he is being healed by the Lord of a second chance. Not once but three times he stood by the [charcoal] fire and denied his Lord; not once but three times he stands by the fire and professes his love. Jesus says to Peter, Jesus says to everyone who's ever stood by the fire and failed God, Jesus says still to you and me whatever we've done, "Get back in the game. Nurture the gifts I gave you and cherish the calling I gave you and devote yourself to the church. Feed my sheep. They need you." (*Love Beyond Reason*, 68–69)

Just as Peter worked through failure to a new understanding of his relationship with Jesus, so we too have the opportunity to hear God speak to us about who we are. Begin by writing down seven good things about yourself and seven bad things. These can be physical, emotional, mental, or whatever. This practical idea comes from Michael Wilkins (see *In His Image*, 81–88).

Good Things About Yourself	Bad Things About Yourself
1.	1.
2.	2.
3.	3.
4.	4.
5.	5.
6.	6.
7.	7.

Wilkins says that knowing ourselves is a good place to start developing our identity in Christ. He encourages us to avoid the trap of comparing ourselves with others and go ahead and accept ourselves—"OK, like everyone else, I have some good and some bad. I'm not going to focus on either one. Instead, I trust God to use my strengths and transform my weaknesses by the power of his Spirit." Wilkins suggests that we *build on the good* and *grow away from the bad*" by absorbing the truth of Scripture, forgetting about ourselves, connecting with God's community, and going public with our new identity.

Why not check out what God says about who you are "in Christ." (Some of you hate to look up verses, but you do other things that you hate, like shaving, so give this a try.) What do these Scriptures say about our new identity in Christ?

- John 1:12–13

- Romans 6:23; 1 Corinthians 15:22; 1 Thessalonians 4:16

- Romans 8:1

- Romans 8:38–39

- Romans 12:5; Galatians 3:28

- 1 Corinthians 1:2

- 1 Corinthians 1:4; Ephesians 2:7; 2 Timothy 1:9; 2:1

- 2 Corinthians 3:14

- 2 Corinthians 5:19; Ephesians 2:13

- Galatians 2:4

- Galatians 2:16

- Galatians 2:20; Colossians 3:3–4

- Galatians 3:26

- Ephesians 1:3

Stop Comparing!
Even after Peter had been restored by Jesus, Peter had the nerve to start comparing himself with John, another follower. Jesus tells Peter to stop it—"Jesus answered, 'If I want him [John] to remain alive until I return, what is that to you? You [Peter] must follow me'" (John 21:22). Are you always comparing yourself with other people? The same people? Why do you do it? God hates comparison because somebody always loses when we compare. How can you stop comparing?

- Ephesians 1:11

- Ephesians 1:13

- Ephesians 2:10

- Ephesians 4:32

- Philippians 3:9

- Philippians 4:7; 1 Peter 5:14

- Colossians 2:9–10

- 2 Timothy 2:1

- 1 Peter 1:23; 2:9

So What?

1. Jesus used Simon Peter's failure to help Peter understand who he really was. Have you ever given your failures to God? What other life circumstances has God used most effectively to shape your identity?

2. Of all the Scriptures that describe our new identity in Christ, which ones are the most meaningful to you at this point in your life? Why?

3. As you think about the good and bad things you wrote about your-self, can you think of a few specific ways to "build on the good and grow from the bad"?

4. Read the quote from Boyd in the sidebar on page 62. In essence the apostle Paul is saying, "Be who you are." Why is it important that God always sees our behavior arising from our identity and not the other way around?

5. What has helped you more than anything else to see yourself as the new person you are in Christ?

6. How can the members of your community group help each other embrace their new identity in Christ and live accordingly?

Cross-References
See the list of "in Christ" verses on pages 61–62.

For Deeper Study
Ortberg, John. *Love Beyond Reason: Moving God's Love from Your Head to Your Heart.* Grand Rapids: Zondervan, 1998.
Stott, John. *Life in Christ.* Wheaton, IL: Tyndale House, 1991.
Wilkins, Michael J. *In His Image: Reflecting Christ in Everyday Life.* Colorado Springs: NavPress, 1997.

WORKS CITED ■ ■ ■ ■ ■

Blomberg, Craig L. *Matthew*. New American Commentary. Nashville: Broadman & Holman, 1992.

Bonhoeffer, Dietrich. *The Cost of Discipleship*. New York: Macmillan, 1963.

Boyd, Gregory A. *Repenting of Religion: Turning from Judgment to the Love of God*. Grand Rapids: Baker, 2004.

Bruner, Frederick Dale. *The Christbook: Matthew 1–12*. Grand Rapids: Eerdmans, 1987.

Duvall, J. Scott, and J. Daniel Hays. *Grasping God's Word: A Hands-On Approach to Reading, Interpreting, and Applying the Bible*. 2nd ed. Grand Rapids: Zondervan, 2005.

Edwards, Dwight. *Revolution Within: A Fresh Look at Supernatural Living*. New York: Random House, 2001.

Erickson, Millard J. *The Concise Dictionary of Christian Theology*. Wheaton: Crossway, 2001.

Garland, David E. *Mark*. NIV Application Commentary. Grand Rapids: Zondervan, 1996.

Guinness, Os. *The Call: Finding and Fulfilling the Central Purpose of Your Life*. Nashville: Word, 1998.

Keener, Craig S. *A Commentary on the Gospel of Matthew*. Grand Rapids: Eerdmans, 1999.

Kidner, Derek. *Genesis*. Tyndale Old Testament Commentary. Downers Grove, IL: InterVarsity Press, 1982.

Lewis, C. S. *Mere Christianity*. New York: Macmillan, 1952.

————. *The Screwtape Letters*. New York: Macmillan, 1961.

————. *The Weight of Glory*. 1949. San Francisco: HarperSanFrancisco, 1980.

Long, Jimmy. *Emerging Hope: Strategy for Reaching Postmodern Generations*. 2nd ed. Downers Grove, IL: InterVarsity Press, 2004.

Manning, Brennan. *The Wisdom of Tenderness: What Happens When God's Fierce Mercy Transforms Our Lives*. San Francisco: Harper San Francisco, 2004.

Ortberg, John. *Love Beyond Reason: Moving God's Love From Your Head to Your Heart*. Grand Rapids: Zondervan, 1998.

Plantinga, Cornelius. *Not the Way It's Supposed to Be: A Breviary of Sin*. Grand Rapids: Eerdmans, 1995.

Sittser, Gerald L. *The Will of God as a Way of Life: Finding and Following the Will of God*. Grand Rapids: Zondervan, 2000.

Smedes, Lewis B. *The Art of Forgiving*. New York: Random House, 1997.

Stott, John R. W. *Basic Christianity*. Grand Rapids: Eerdmans, 1986.

————. *The Message of the Sermon on the Mount*. The Bible Speaks Today. Downers Grove, IL: InterVarsity Press, 1978.

Swenson, Richard A. *Margin*. Colorado Springs: NavPress, 1992.

Thomas à Kempis. *Imitation of Christ*. Notre Dame, IN: Ave Maria Press, 1989.

Warren, Rick. *The Purpose-Driven Life*. Grand Rapids: Zondervan, 2002.

Webster, Doug. *The Easy Yoke*. Colorado Springs: NavPress, 1995.

Wilkins, Michael J. *In His Image: Reflecting Christ in Everyday Life*. Colorado Springs, NavPress, 1997.

Willard, Dallas. *Renovation of the Heart*. Colorado Springs: NavPress, 2002.

Yancey, Philip. *The Jesus I Never Knew*. Grand Rapids: Zondervan, 1995.